FEASTING WITH THE TRINITY

*A Formative Approach to
Growing in Godliness*

KENDELL EASLEY

FEASTING WITH THE TRINITY
Copyright © 2019 **Kendell Easley**

All rights reserved. No part of this book may be used or reproduced by any means, graphic, electronic, or mechanical, including photocopying, recording, taping or by information storage and retrieval system without the written permission of the author except in the case of brief quotations embodied in critical articles and reviews.

Stratton Press Publishing,
831 N Tatnall Street Suite M #188,
Wilmington, DE 19801
www.stratton-press.com
1-888-323-7009

[Bible translation information as required; all Scripture quotes are from the Christian Standard Bible, 2017]

Because of the dynamic nature of the Internet, any web addresses or links contained in this book may have changed since publication and may no longer be valid. The views expressed in the work are solely those of the author and do not necessarily reflect the views of the publisher, and the publisher hereby disclaims any responsibility for them.

Any people depicted in stock imagery provided by Shutterstock are models, and such images are being used for illustrative purposes only.

ISBN (Paperback): 978-1-64345-629-4
ISBN (Ebook): 978-1-64345-630-0

Printed in the United States of America

Dedicated to the glory of God
and in grateful appreciation
to the three institutions of higher education
in which I have had the privilege
of serving as professor:
Toccoa Falls College,
Mid-America Baptist Theological Seminary,
and
Union University

CONTENTS

INTRODUCTION..7

Part 1. BREAKFAST WITH THE FATHER, OR BIBLICAL FORMATION............................13

DOXOLOGY
(Breakfast with the Father) 15

WORLDVIEW
(Breakfast with the Father) 27

THEOLOGY
(Breakfast with the Father) 39

SCRIPTURE
(Breakfast with the Father) 53

Part 2. LUNCH WITH THE SPIRIT OR SPRITUAL FORMATION 67

SPIRITUAL POWER
(Lunch with the Spirit)..69

SPIRITUAL FRUIT
(Lunch with the Spirit)..81

SPIRITUAL HEALTH
(Lunch with the Spirit) 95

SPIRITUAL DISCIPLINE
(Lunch with the Spirit) 107

**Part 3. SUPPER WITH THE SON, OR
RELATIONAL FORMATION 119**

WORSHIP IN COMMUNITY
(Supper with the Son) 121

COMPANIONSHIP IN COMMUNITY
(Supper with the Son) 133

MISSION IN COMMUNITY
(Supper with the Son) 145

SERVICE IN COMMUNITY
(Supper with the Son) 159

INTRODUCTION

I am journeying through life as an American, male, Caucasian, and baby-boomer, all of which are mine because of the circumstances of my birth. Given the state of contemporary culture, let me add that I have never thought of choosing a different identity for any of these factors. Further, even though this individuality has shaped me in ways I can never escape, I have always benefited greatly from those who live from an entirely different identity. Further, I have written this book, as intentionally as I possibly can, not only for "my kind of people" but also for non-Americans, females, people of color, and those of generations both younger and older than me.

    I have deliberately chosen to live as a follower of Jesus, a Christian who takes the gospel seriously. Yet throughout my adult years I have been struck by how many diverse and bewildering options have claimed to be "the way" to Christlikeness. Pietism, the spiritual disciplines, Catholic mysticism, neo-Puritanism, missional community, and charismatic experience are a few such approaches. I have tried out several of these models. For example, I look back with fondness on my three-year charismatic phase in the 1970s. The neo-Reformed, neo-Puritan resurgence of the 1990s captured my attention. More recently, in the 2010s I was part of a contemporary church plant that emphasized missional community as the best expression for Christian living. Then came an unexpected academic assignment to teach spiritual formation at the graduate level, which threw me into a new realm of reflecting on the classic spiritual disciplines. The highlight of that season was my participation in a silent retreat at the Abbey of Gethsemani, Thomas Merton's monastery in Kentucky.

All this left me in a sanctification muddle. I asked myself, "Are there supposed to be so many competing models, each of which claims to be the best way to grow in Christlikeness?" And indeed, Kenneth Boa's work, *Conformed to His Image*, does a terrific job of showing how such models may be thought of as various facets, as he calls them, of Christian growth.

Then relief and clarity came to me from two unexpected directions. First is the recently renewed emphasis on the Trinity among Christian thinkers, for example *The Deep Things of God: How the Trinity Changes Everything* by Fred Sanders. The Trinity is so much more than just another theological ingredient for Christianity. When rightly understood, the Trinity is the essential reality daily impacting our lives. An "aha!" moment came when I grasped the notion of dancing with the Trinity as articulated by Larry Crabb in *Soul Talk* and in his School of Spiritual Direction, in which I participated for a refreshing week in October 2015.

Second, a foray into Scripture brought a fresh realization that eating—feasting—is one of the grand themes woven throughout the biblical materials, yet often overlooked. Our first parents chose to eat the forbidden food. The Israelites feasted on lamb and unleavened bread at the beginning of their redemption. They were sustained by manna for forty years. Three annual festivals became part of Israel's rhythm of life. Solomon's magnificence was illustrated by the bounty of his daily table. "Ezekiel 4:9 Bread" remains a fascination. Jesus's miracles sometimes featured abundant food or drink. He instituted the Lord's Supper with bread and wine. After his resurrection, he ate with his disciples more than once.

All these examples involve real, physical eating. Some of them also include a figurative or spiritual meaning, such as the fruit in Eden, the food of Passover, and Communion. Then there are texts in which eating is meant mainly (or only) in spiritual terms, such as these:

- He gave you manna to eat, which you and your fathers had not known, so that you might learn that man does not live on bread alone but on every word that comes from the mouth of the LORD. (Deut 8:3)
- How sweet your word is to my taste—sweeter than honey in my mouth. (Ps 119:103)

- I tell you that many will come from east and west to share the banquet with Abraham, Isaac, and Jacob in the kingdom of heaven. (Matt 8:11)
- Then he said to me, "Write: Blessed are those invited to the marriage feast of the Lamb!" He also said to me, "These words of God are true." (Rev 19:9)

The book before you presents "feasting with the Trinity" as a grand metaphor for living and enjoying the Christian life. Formation in godliness can well be understood as responding to God's invitation to feast with Father, Son, and Spirit. We also dine with others belonging to the people of God. As we partake of what God sets on his table, feasting with him and with others, we are formed over a lifetime into Christlike persons.

Breakfast with the Father, or Biblical Formation

Growing in godliness begins with understanding and developing a relationship with the Father. We seek to be oriented properly to our Creator (doxological focus) as well as to the world we inhabit as his creatures (attending to worldview foundations). We are then able to understand and embrace essential themes in Christian teaching (theological concepts) as well as God's story (biblical content). Come enjoy breakfast.

Lunch with the Spirit, or Spiritual Formation

Sanctification moves forward only as the Spirit enables us. We seek and enjoy the fullness of the indwelling Spirit, including his gifts and his fruit. With the Spirit's help, we arrive at greater emotional health (such as restoration from brokenness caused by anger, shame, or fear). Often the Spirit uses the classic spiritual disciplines, sometimes called the means of grace, to accomplish his work in individuals. Let's eat lunch every day.

Supper with the Son, or Relational Formation

Christian maturity is impossible in isolation. The church is Christ's body; he is the head of the body. We therefore worship with others, demonstrating the community of Jesus (among whom Communion enacts feasting with the Trinity). Along the way, we may be especially helped by sacred friendships, companions journeying with us toward Christlikeness. Yet we are called not to stay in our enclaves; rather, we have been sent into the world to make disciples. Following the great commandments means that we practice living sacrificially for others, including involvement in social justice issues. Supper is served.

PART 1

BREAKFAST WITH THE FATHER, OR BIBLICAL FORMATION

Growing in godliness begins with understanding and developing a relationship with our heavenly Father. The "breakfast focus" is on those parts of our growth that see the Father as the revealer of truth. Here's what's on the menu.

Doxology. We understand our journey to Christlikeness best when we recognize that the process and the goal are God's glory: his weightiness or worthiness. When we grasp that glorifying God is the only sure path to genuine happiness and flourishing, then we will want to journey with this magnificent objective in view.

Worldview. As followers of Jesus, we are to be committed intentionally to the essentials of a biblical worldview, which can no longer be taken for granted. We need to think about God as the primary reality, ourselves as created in God's image, and truth and morality as anchored in God, who does not lie and has revealed truth and morality through Scripture.

Theology. Growth in sanctification includes increasing our understanding of what the Bible teaches about essential topics. We may feast on countless facets of theology at various points throughout our lives. Yet we may begin by focusing on the classic topics of theology: God himself, Scripture, humanity, Christ, salvation, the church, and last things.

Scripture. Scripture is the Word of God in the words of men. Thus, we need to learn the grand story the Bible tells. Further, we are to practice disciplined Bible study, seeking both the original meaning and the contemporary significance of a text. Further, we can practice sacred reading of a text, seeking to be shaped by the Word rather than merely informed by it.

DOXOLOGY (BREAKFAST WITH THE FATHER)

The journey of godliness has the glory of God as its beginning, its process, and its end. The theme of God's glory echoes throughout both the Old Testament and the New. The Westminster Shorter Catechism (1647), highly influential among English-speaking Christians, famously began by asking, "What is the chief end of man?" The answer: "Man's chief end is to glorify God, and to enjoy him forever."

"Doxology," literally "an expression of glory," recalls a classic hymn beginning, "Praise God from whom all blessings flow." Yet there is much more to doxology than repeating a liturgical utterance. When we grasp—or rather are grasped by—the truth that the path toward Christlikeness means living in the light of his glory, then we have well begun. Without this foundation, our journey will short-circuit and may end up as a hodge-podge of techniques.

The Glory of God in the Old Testament

The main word translated "glory" in Hebrew Scripture is kabod. Its root idea is that something or someone is heavy or weighty and therefore worthy. Thus, wealthy or honorable humans had glory. Mainly, however, kabod in the Bible refers to God's worthiness, that is, his matchless honor and admirable reputation. Thus, "the whole earth is filled with the Lord's glory" (Num 14:21). Habakkuk longed for the day when "the earth will be filled with the knowledge of the Lord's glory, as the waters cover the sea" (Hab 2:14). God's glory—like his name—is one way of summarizing his greatness and goodness, everything that he is.

God's glory also refers to the visible light or brilliance that he often surrounds himself with when he reveals himself. Light was God's first creation; perhaps this is why he discloses himself by means of light. Thus, the brightness of God filled the Israelites' tabernacle and later their temple. The prophet Ezekiel strained to describe God's glory: "The appearance of the brilliant light all around was like that of a rainbow in a cloud on a rainy day. This was the appearance of the likeness of the Lord's glory" (Ezek 1:28).

The frequent expressions of praise found throughout the Psalms, notably "hallelujah" or "praise the Lord," are surely statements or commands to glorify God, that is, to acknowledge fully his superlative worth. The Latin-writing Christian thinker Augustine summarized God's glory as clara notitia cum laude, brilliant celebrity with praise.

The Glory of God in the New Testament

When Scripture was translated into Greek in the time between the Testaments, Jewish scholars used the Greek term doxa to render kabod. The apostles and other writers of the New Testament continued this usage. Thus, the shepherds of Bethlehem were terrified by the glory of the Lord flashing around them (Luke 2:9). Stephen referred to "the God of glory" (Acts 7:2).

New Testament writers also extend glory to Jesus. His is the superior honor: "The Son is the radiance of God's glory and the exact expression of his nature" (Heb 1:3). On one occasion, "his clothes became dazzling white," and Moses and Elijah "appeared in glory" with him (Luke 9:29, 31). Glory is the essence of Jesus's return. He will come "on the clouds of heaven with power and great glory" (Matt 24:30; see also Matt 25:31; Rev 21:23).

The Call to Doxology

"That's the best apple pie I've ever tasted!" "What a stunning performance of Mozart!" "Your face is so wonderful! I could never tire of gazing into your eyes!" When we experience something or someone good or true or beautiful, we can't help but offer admiration. We naturally overflow with praise. We are suspicious of a man who claims to have discovered his one true love and yet keeps it to himself. We want him to write a poem or put it on social media, somehow to let the world know. This goes all the way back to Adam's whoop: "This one, at last, is bone of my bone and flesh of my flesh" (Gen 2:23).

Worship means offering glory and praise to God, the one who is most highly valued. (Worship, or offering highest praise, to something or someone other than God is the essence of idolatry.) Thus, when Moses saw God's visible glory in the burning bush, he worshiped and hid his face (Exod 3). Ultimately, he led an entire nation to experience God's glory and to become a worshiping people. Centuries later Isaiah saw the exalted Lord and acknowledged his own unworthiness (Isa 6). He later proclaimed messages both of challenge and of comfort. There are also commands to glorify—worship, praise, love, fear—God.

- Love the LORD your God with all your heart, with all your soul, and with all your strength. (Deut 6:5; see Matt 22:35–38)
- You are to fear the LORD your God and worship him. Remain faithful to him and take oaths in his name. He is your praise and he is your God. (Deut 10:20–21)

One surprise, perhaps, about Jesus in the Gospels was his willingness to receive expressions of divine worship and love and praise from others (for example, Matt 21:9, 15–16; Luke 7:47; John 9:38; 21:15–17). In the Epistles and Revelation, glorifying Jesus—worshiping, loving, enjoying him—is the main business of his followers.

- God highly exalted him and gave him the name that is above every name, so that at the name of Jesus every knee will bow . . . and every tongue will confess. (Phil 2:9–11)
- Though you have not seen him, you love him; though not seeing him now, you believe in him, and you rejoice with inexpressible and glorious joy. (1 Pet 1:8)
- Worthy is the Lamb who was slaughtered to receive power and riches and wisdom and strength and honor and glory and blessing! (Rev 5:11; see also 7:9–10)

Motives for Doxology

It's one thing to agree that God is glorious and that he has revealed his glory. After all, he is God. He is the greatest. Many, however, ask: Why does God want to be praised so badly? Isn't it selfish of God to hog the glory for himself? After all, didn't Paul write that genuine love "is not boastful; is not arrogant" (1 Cor 13:4)? When we think about it, the incentives for building our lives on the foundation of glorifying God are threefold. First are motives that spring from God himself: his essence and his actions. Second are motives based on who we are as humans. Third is the impact of our glorifying God on the rest of creation.

Motives for doxology based in God himself. If it is right to praise the praiseworthy, then it should be evident that because God is the best, we should acknowledge that this is true. God is to be glorified because of who he is. If there is some Being greater than the biblically revealed God—more powerful, for example, or more loving—then two things are immediately apparent. First, the biblical God is no longer God. Second, we should acknowledge that other Being with highest praise. Because God is the greatest, however, it falls on us to say so.

Glorifying God is also what we do when we recall what he has done. He has created and he has redeemed. We will praise God when we recall that he has given us our very existence. "Acknowledge that the Lord is God. He made us, and we are his. . . . Enter his gates with thanksgiving and his courts with praise" (Ps 100:3–4). Further, he has provided salvation for us at the cost of his Son. How should those who understand the meaning of salvation respond? Peter stated it this way: "You are a chosen race, a royal priesthood, a holy nation, a people for his possession, so that you may proclaim the praises of the one who called you out of darkness into his marvelous light" (1 Pet 2:9).

Motives for doxology based in ourselves. We fulfill the purpose for which we were created and redeemed when we intentionally glorify God. As a parallel, consider a magnificent racecar—or if you prefer, a wonderful grand piano—which was designed, built, suffered a terrible accident, and then was rebuilt.

How will the car best fulfill its purpose? By racing, of course. It might be used as a taxi or a vehicle for an urban commute, but how sad if it does not race. How will the piano best fulfill its reason for being built and then restored? Not by serving as dust catcher in the living room. It needs to be played to fulfill its purpose. How sad when we squander the reason God lavished attention on us: to bring attention to him and to his glory. Why would we short-circuit the purpose for which we were created?

A second reason within ourselves for glorifying God is that this is the only sure way to a life of human flourishing. Throughout the ages philosophers and great religious minds alike have pondered the essence of what it means to be fulfilled as a human being. Is human fulfillment found in seeking a life of virtue, as Aristotle and other ancient Greeks taught? What about a life of helping others? Might the highest and best life be found in indulging the senses? (Recall the frustrated ponderings of the author of Ecclesiastes, who failed to flourish despite so many experiments.) Does the maximum expression of personal freedom—the current Western favorite "ethical" value—grant happiness?

The right answer is "none of the above." There's something much better than a life either of self-centeredness or of others-centeredness. Life focused on God and seeking to honor him is commended throughout Scripture and the history of the church as the best possible life. The Psalmist wrote, "You reveal the path of life to me; in your presence is abundant joy; in your right hand are eternal pleasures" (Ps 16:11). In his autobiography Augustine wrote: "You stir mankind to take pleasure in praising you, because you have made us for yourself, and our heart is restless until it rests in you" (Confessions, I, 1, i).

Motives for doxology based in others. There is a third kind of motive to glorify God above all else. Jesus taught those who belong to him how to live as citizens of his kingdom. Among his startling teachings: "Let your light shine before others, so that they may see your good works and give glory to your Father in heaven" (Matt 5:16). No one doubts that believers are called on to do works of mercy and to seek for social justice. But such charity is not biblical if it does not point to the God who inspires loving service. It is not fighting for dignity and freedom from oppression per se that we do what we do. We do so to show others the God who has called us to be such persons and to live such lives.

Further, our verbal witness to the good news—evangelism, sharing our faith—is even more obviously a way to glorify God. When persons hear the gospel proclaimed and repent and believe, God is glorified. Again, Jesus pointed the way: "There is joy in the presence of God's angels over one sinner who repents" (Luke 15:10; see Rev 7:9-10).

Seeking Our Own Glory as Humans

Almost everyone enjoys being recognized for a job well done. Many of us have an urge to compete and win a prize. It's important to think clearly about the relationship between exercising our ambition (as we use God-given talents and creativity) versus seeking to glorify God in all things. Put simply, Scripture makes a large place for us to seek to excel, yet at the same time God's people are warned repeatedly against the sin of pride. Self-exaltation is the fountainhead from which other sins flow.

Scripture overflows with examples of human excellence. Bezalel was uniquely gifted and blessed as the supervisor in crafting the Israelites' tabernacle (Exod 31:1–11). David excelled both as a warrior and as a poet. Blessed with natural loveliness, Esther won a beauty contest and used all her skills to save her people from extinction.

In a variety of contexts Paul supported the efforts of persons (including himself) to do their best and make plans to succeed. Consider the following:

- I have strongly desired for many years to come to you. (Rom 15:23)
- I discipline my body and bring it under strict control. (1 Cor 9:27)
- I pursue as my goal the prize promised by God's heavenly call in Christ Jesus. (Phil 3:14)
- Brothers and sisters, do not grow weary in doing good. (2 Thess 3:13)
- If anyone aspires to be an overseer, he desires a noble work. (1 Tim 3:1)

What is striking about these passages is that the emphasis is not on the one striving; rather, the focus is on the impact such effort will have on the kingdom of God. Paul didn't commend those who seek praise for themselves. Only occasionally did he acknowledge the value of praising others because of their praiseworthy deeds (Rom 13:7).

Biblical religion, in contrast to other religions or philosophies, is unique in its condemnation of pride and its commendation of humility. The essence of pride is refusing to depend on God and submit to him. Pride attributes to self the honor and glory due to God. Some have argued that pride was first revealed when Satan attempted to set his throne above God's throne (see Isa 14:12–14). The Old Testament consistently condemns pride; Psalms and Proverbs offer a sustained critique of arrogance: "Pride comes before destruction, and an arrogant spirit before a fall" (Prov 16:18). This is unlike the Greek philosophers, who promoted pride as a virtue and humility as despicable.

The New Testament writers reject the Greek view in favor of the Old Testament view. The basis for this was Jesus's own life of humility, refusing any self-assertion. His self-claim was that he was "lowly and humble in heart" (Matt 11:29). He condemned pride as an evil that defiles (Mark 7:22). One of his memorable parables, about the Pharisee and the tax collector, depicted those guilty of spiritual pride (Luke 18:9). The longest meditation on Christ's humility is Paul's declaration in Philippians 2, including this astonishing teaching: "He humbled himself by becoming obedient to the point of death—even to death on a cross" (Phil 2:8).

Our difficulty as human beings—whether following Jesus intentionally or not—is that we are self-seeking creatures. We are right to celebrate the achievements of others, and we may seek to excel in using the talents and gifts God has provided. Yet our desires to achieve and our pleasure at being recognized for success are always to be tempered. Thus C. S. Lewis noted, "Since to be famous means to be better known than other people, the desire for fame appears to me as a competitive passion and therefore of hell rather than heaven" ("The Weight of Glory," preached June 8, 1941). We need others around us to help keep our pride in check. We are meant to join Paul when he wrote, "As for me, I will never boast about anything except the cross of our Lord Jesus Christ" (Gal 6:14).

"Those He justified, He also Glorified"

As Christ's followers, we cannot rightly seek our own glory, but we certainly look forward to hearing our Master affirm us: "Well done, good and faithful servant!" (Matt 25:23). Experiencing God's pleasure over us is surely the greatest joy imaginable.

Whatever the joys of heaven will be—the final state of believers after the return of Christ—they are associated with receiving an imperishable resurrection body. In the apostle Paul's reasoning, Jesus's resurrection guarantees the future resurrection of believers. He saw this as so certain that he referred to receiving the resurrection body as a done deal: "Those he justified, he also glorified" (Rom 8:30).

We have begun thinking about our journey toward godliness with reflections on the glory of God as the beginning, middle, and end of the journey. God's glory is a central feature of Scripture; the call for God's people to give him—the Triune God—glory is pervasive, as are the biblical teachings about the motives and the means for glorifying him in all things. In our desires to achieve, we are encouraged; yet we are warned not to let pride—taking glory for ourselves that belongs only to God—lead us astray. We seek to worship humbly, knowing that sin and death will be destroyed forever when we receive our glorified bodies.

Reflective Questions

- How confident are you that the only sure path for personal happiness is to glorify God?
- How clear is the biblical teaching that the glory of God is the center of all things?
- What steps or life changes might you consider taking so that your life is ordered around glorifying God and enjoying him forever?

WORLDVIEW (BREAKFAST WITH THE FATHER)

If you have read the first chapter, you may be thinking, "Wait a minute! It's all well and good to talk about God and his glory. But aren't you assuming something about the existence of God and what he is like?" You are right. We need to be clear what our assumptions are about God and the nature of reality. Who or what is God? Can we know truth? Can we ever be sure of what is right and wrong? These are worldview questions. So, what is your worldview?

Worldview (a translation from the German *Weltanschauung,* a combination of *Welt,* "world," and *Anschauung*, "outlook" or "perspective") has been widely discussed by philosophers—non-Christians as well as Christians of various theological persuasions—for over a century. James Sire's *The Universe Next Door: A Basic Worldview Catalog* has been most helpful in identifying worldviews competing for attention in our world today. He also helped frame the questions which worldviews must answer.

What is a Worldview and Why Does It Matter?

Worldview matters because everyone operates from a set of assumptions. These may be consciously held or only subconscious, and they may be true or false. We all live according to some core beliefs about reality. Somehow, for example, we assume that we are real persons (not just dreaming that we are real) and that the ground will hold us up when we get out of bed. Without a worldview, conscious or not, true or false, action is impossible.

So, on the silly end of worldview (at least to me it's silly) is the delightfully absurd worldview expressed by the Queen in *Alice in Wonderland:* "'There's no use trying,' she [Alice] said. 'One can't believe impossible things.' 'I daresay you haven't had much practice,' said the Queen. 'When I was your age, I always did it for half-an-hour a day. Why, sometimes I've believed as many as six impossible things before breakfast.'"

On the serious side of worldview, for sixteen centuries confessing Christians around the world have affirmed the opening of the Nicene Creed. Its assumptions may seem as absurd, to many people today, as the Queen's claim: "We believe in one God, the Father almighty, maker of heaven and earth, of all things visible and invisible. And in one Lord Jesus Christ, the only Son of God, begotten from the

Father before all ages, God from God, Light from Light, true God from true God, begotten, not made; of the same essence as the Father."

So, it makes a huge difference if persons base their understanding of reality on God the Creator and Jesus as his Son, or if they believe—as apparently many postmodern persons do—that everything is so relative that believing six impossible things before breakfast is the way to go: "Well, that may be true for you, but it's not true for me."

Before we sketch the elements of a worldview, it will helpful to cite Sire's definition: "A worldview is a commitment, a fundamental orientation of the heart, that can be expressed as a story or in a set of presuppositions (assumptions which may be true, partially true or entirely false) that we hold (consciously or subconsciously, consistently or inconsistently) about the basic constitution of reality, and that provides the foundation on which we live and move and have our being" (2009, p. 20). To unpack this statement is beyond the scope of this chapter. But the connection between maintaining a worthwhile worldview and growing in godliness becomes clear when you recognize that worldview answers matters of ultimate importance.

The Big Questions Any Worldview Should Answer

What is the primary reality? This question concerns whether god or gods exist, and if so, what he or it or they are like and are capable of. Religious worldviews by definition posit a divinity—perhaps the Trinity of Christianity or Allah of Islam or the multiple gods of Hinduism. Non-religious worldviews may deny any deity or posit uncertainty.

What are human beings? Are we the product of millions of years of random selection and survival of the fittest? Is there a special place for humanity on earth? That is, are human beings exceptional and superior to the rest of earth's inhabitants? Are we here because of a divine plan (by an intelligent designer or by direct creation or some other way)?

Why and how can truth be known, or is this even possible? In philosophical inquiry, this is called epistemology, but don't let the formal name frighten you. Is truth something we humans figure out by observation and experience (empiricism)? Or is knowledge based in reason (rationalism)? Or has God (or the gods) made truth knowable through revelation—either supernatural or natural? Or perhaps truth is neither possible nor desirable.

What is the basis for understanding good and evil, right and wrong? Ethics refers to a code of conduct provided by an external source (for instance, workplace ethics or ethics of the nursing profession). Morals refers to someone's personal principles of right and wrong, whether consistently applied or not. Where do such ideas come from? Do we base them on God or a holy book or conscience or cultural consensus or what?

What is the purpose of history generally and of individuals particularly? When we say "it was meant to be" or "things will turn out all right," we are affirming that our lives matter beyond ourselves. So, is human history going anywhere? Is there a goal? Can evil and suffering (personal or endured by many) be purposeful? Will evil ultimately be avenged? Is there an afterlife? How real are heaven and hell?

Worldviews Based on God or Religion

Before looking more closely at the worldview upon which growth in godliness can flourish, let's sketch a few alternate worldviews having a measurable impact in today's developed countries. We begin with two worldviews based on a deity.

Islam. Since the 9/11 tragedy, we in the Western world have become much more aware that Islam is an influential presence. While public debate has raged about the nature of Islam (a religion of peace?), certainly Islam's foundational assumptions are vastly different from—and incompatible with—Christianity. It's impossible to be equally Muslim and Christian.

For Muslims, the primary reality is Allah, a deity who is decidedly not the Trinity affirmed by Christians. In Islam, humanity is believed to be created by God, and truth as well as right and wrong are based on the teachings of the Qur'an. Muslim scholars, either of the Sunni or the Shi'a branches, provide interpretation of the Qur'an and guidance for followers. The ethical system of Islam includes a desire for all humans to be ruled by Sharia law. The purpose of history is for all people to live under Islam, and this is fostered by Jihad.

A great question that demonstrates the incompatibility of the worldviews of Islam and confessional Christianity is this: Is the God of Muhammed the Father of Jesus Christ? Neither orthodox Christians nor committed Muslims will legitimately answer this question yes.

Moralistic therapeutic deism (MTD). In 2005 sociologists Christian Smith and Melinda Lundquist Denton released their findings in a study of some 3000 teenagers, the "National Study of Youth and Religion." Their book, Soul Searching: The Religious and Spiritual Lives of American Teenagers, has received a great deal of attention. They found that many young people have embraced MTD as a workable informal set of assumptions on which to base life. These presuppositions are a diluted amalgamation of understandings about God and morality that are not actually taught in any major world religion. Here are five premises on which followers of MTD base their approach to life:

- God created and ordered the world and watches over human life on earth.
- God wants people to be good, nice, and fair to each other, as taught in the Bible and by most world religions.
- The central goal of life is to be happy and to feel good about oneself.

- God does not need to be particularly involved in one's life except when he is needed to resolve a problem.
- Good people go to heaven when they die.

MTD is a worldview. It answers the question of human origins as well as the afterlife. It speaks about the purpose of life right now, assuming that the moral tenets of the world's religions are alike. MTD also thinks of God as merely the great problem solver. One glaring weakness of MTD is its fostering of self-centeredness and self-expression. It fits nicely with the typical intentions of many governments: government exists to secure and protect the maximum freedom of personal expression for individuals.

Worldviews Not Based on God or Religion

Secular humanism. The medieval synthesis of understanding reality based on divine revelation was challenged first by the Renaissance (1300s–1500s). The humanities rather than divinity were what made the influencers passionate. The Enlightenment (1700s) swept through Europe and America, ushering in the Age of Reason and proving the value of the scientific method. Both the American Revolution (1776) and the French Revolution (1789) were largely Enlightenment products.

In the 1800s the push toward humanism raced ahead through four towering figures:

- Charles Darwin (1809–82) developed a theory of natural evolution requiring no Creator.
- Karl Marx (1818–83) viewed economics and politics as class struggle with no place for God.
- Friedrich Nietzsche (1844–1900) asserted nihilism (meaninglessness) and the death of God.
- Sigmund Freud (1856–1939) invented psychoanalysis as a way of understanding and treating human beings without reference to God.

In the last half of the twentieth century, Western intellectuals became increasingly secular. Religion was no longer assumed as normative or having a direct impact. "Is God Dead?" *Time* screamed from its April 8, 1966, cover. Evolution and psychoanalysis triumphed. Various versions of the *Humanist Manifesto* laid out beliefs and agendas. Secular humanists accept only natural science as a source for truth; they are increasingly influential in promoting a "progressive" agenda in areas such as human sexuality. Without God, no afterlife is possible.

Postmodernism. It was only a matter of time until the supposed certainties of science were challenged. Truth began to be thought of as personal and subjective rather than universal. The right of *homo sapiens* to occupy a superior place on earth was questioned. Albert Einstein (1879–1955) is widely considered the most influential intellectual of the twentieth century. His theory of relativity posited that space and time are not constant. If so, then it was inevitable for extreme forms of relativism to develop.

Postmodern thinking is skeptical of certainty and suspicious of almost everything. Irony rules. Some theorists argued that truth is simply a matter of manipulating language. Truth has become a matter of personal interpretation. It's all personal perception and emphatic subjectivity. The triumph of the internet and social media means every postmodern instinct finds supporters. "Whatever!" and "true for you but not for me" are postmodern clichés. For postmodern persons, ethnicity and gender have become matters of personal preference and have little (or nothing) to do with scientifically provable facts. In its April 3, 2017, cover story, *Time* asked, "Is Truth Dead?"

Elements of a Confessional Worldview

The worldviews noted above greatly influence contemporary culture. Together they have toppled Christianity from its previously secure position of privilege. The result of the Renaissance, the Age of Reason, the humanism that took root in the 1800s, and the current turn toward postmodern radical relativism will not end well. All such views founder because they have rejected the God of the Bible and historic forms of Christianity as curious relics. All who intend to grow in godliness need to know that we are now a challenged minority. We hold assumptions that have been fervently and consistently confessed over the centuries. Here are the central presuppositions of a confessional worldview.

God is the infinite, all knowing, good, and loving creator and ruler of all things, existing eternally as three persons, one God: Father, Son, and Spirit. Here is the primary reality. The ancient creeds of Christianity—the Apostles' Creed and the Nicene Creed—begin here and are certainly trinitarian. Scripture famously begins, "In the beginning God created the heavens and the earth" (Gen 1:1). Persons accepting this statement will have no trouble accepting anything else affirmed in the Bible; if they reject this teaching, they are well on the way to rejecting historic Christianity.

Human beings were created in the image of God as morally good but fell into evil and are now marred by sin yet loved by God and capable of redemption and much good. This answers the question, what are human beings? This assumption affirms nothing about the processes God used to create mankind nor about how long humans have existed. If humans have come about by divine action, however, then we are accountable to God for our lives and deeds. Among other things, this view asserts than humans have intelligence (capacity for knowledge and reason), morality (ability to recognize good and evil), and self-determination (ability to make decisions and act). Further, God's creation of humanity included two genders with the possibility of marriage: "So God created man in his own image; he created him in the image of God; he created them male and female" (Gen 1:27).

Truth is possible because it is derived from God who does not lie and who created humankind with the ability to know truth about the world and himself; therefore, all truth is God's truth. Because all humans have fallen into sin, our processes for understanding truth are often flawed. Reason, science, and intuition are not infallible guides. Yet truth may be discovered through special revelation (prophets, Scripture, Jesus Christ) or through natural revelation. Truth is never self-contradictory. Objective truth is possible and desirable. "God is not a man, that he might lie" (Num 23:19). "It is impossible for God to lie" (Heb 6:18). Because Scripture is affirmed as the Word of God, it is trustworthy as a source for truth.

God's standards for morality are revealed in Scripture, and because he is holy and righteous, what he has revealed as right and good is indeed right and good. It is widely believed that all human beings have a conscience, a sense of right and wrong. The source of this sense has been widely debated. For some, "good" is what reason affirms or whatever society says is good or seems to be the greatest good for the greatest number. In a confessional worldview, morals are God-given absolutes, and those who follow Jesus Christ necessarily follow his teachings. "You call me Teacher and Lord—and you are speaking rightly, since that is what I am" (John 13:13). Jesus is the Teacher of Christians, so we believe what he taught; Jesus is the Lord of Christians, so we submit to his commands.

Human history will culminate with the personal, bodily return of Jesus Christ; all humankind will be judged; and each person will live eternally in a glorious existence with God or in terrible sorrow apart from him. The previous chapter (doxology) developed the theme that the chief end of man is to glorify God and enjoy him forever. God plans to bring this final fulfillment about through Christ's return, final judgment, and a re-created heaven and earth. These were implicit in Jesus's insistent teaching about the arrival of the kingdom of God, inaugurated in his first coming and completed at his return. In the words of the Nicene Creed, affirmed weekly by millions, "He will come again in glory to judge the living and the dead, and his kingdom will have no end." In his own words, "When the Son of Man comes in his glory, and all the angels with him, then he will sit on his glorious throne. All the nations will be gathered before him" (Matt 25:31–32).

Reflective Questions

- When did you first learn to think about your worldview?
- How much do you agree that the worldview questions presented are critical for disciples?
- What adjustments in your worldview might need to be made after considering this study?

THEOLOGY (BREAKFAST WITH THE FATHER)

We've thought so far about two "menu items" for our breakfast with the Father in our journey toward godliness. First, our great goal is to glorify God and enjoy him forever. Further, we're challenged to think purposefully about our worldview. Are we committed to the presuppositions that will make our journey profitable and help us reach the desired outcome? We may proceed well only on such a basis.

Now we turn attention to a third "menu item" as we consider that we need to grow in understanding what the Scriptures, our source for revealed truth, teach us. As we learn more and more about these topics ("theology" is the formal term), we will discover that there is more than enough to keep us learning throughout our lives. Indeed, it's my conviction that we'll keep growing in understanding matters of doctrinal truth throughout eternity.

There are many ways to organize theological studies, that is, "What does the whole Bible teach us today about any given topic?" (from Wayne Grudem, *Systematic Theology: An Introduction to Biblical Doctrine,* 1994, 21). In 2006, my more modest work, *52 Words Every Christian Should Know,* organized the major issues of theology around eight controlling ideas: God, Scripture, creation and mankind, sin, Jesus Christ, salvation, the church, and last things. This chapter summarizes the major concerns I dealt with. In the discussion below, I sketch the way forward rather than offer definitive solutions.

God

As growing Christians we presuppose God, revealed in Scripture, as the primary reality. In thinking about God, let's begin with ways in which God is completely unlike us and which we cannot truly comprehend. The "three omnis" come to mind. First is his presence everywhere at all times (*omnipresence*): "Where can I go to escape your Spirit? Where can I flee from your presence? If I go up to heaven, you are there; if I make my bed in Sheol, you are there" (Ps 139:7–8). Second is his knowledge of all things (*omniscience*), with the emphasis on his intimate knowledge of persons: "He counts the number of the stars; he gives names to all of them. Our Lord is great, vast in power; his understanding is infinite" (Ps 147:4–5). Third is his sovereign power (*omnipotence*). He is able to do whatever he wills and he rightfully exercises authority over his creation. He expects human beings to recognize and submit to his rule: "Yours, Lord, is the kingdom, and you are exalted as head over all. Riches and honor come from you, and you are the ruler of everything" (1 Chr 29:11–12).

Next, we can consider ways in which God has shared certain attributes with us human beings. These we can understand, at least to an extent. Because of sin, we are often defective in reflecting these attributes, but growth in godliness means that these are being perfected in us. First is *love*. God exists in a perfect community of love: Father, Son, and Spirit. His love is his freely given, intense affection expressing delight and goodwill to those he loves. *Grace* is his love expressed to those who do not deserve it; *mercy* is his love toward those in need. "God is love, and the one who remains in love remains in God, and God remains in him. . . . We love because he first loved us" (1 John 4:16, 19). Second, his *holiness* comes to mind. Holy means separated. God is like no other; he is morally perfect and righteous. "Holy, holy, holy, Lord God, the Almighty, who was, who is, and who is to come" (Rev 4:8).

Third, we come to God as the *Trinity*. He is one being, yet he exists eternally as three persons: Father, Son, and Spirit. There are not three Gods, but only one. As noted in the chapter on worldview, insistence on God as Trinity undergirds true growth in godliness. In the centuries after Christ's coming, his followers articulated an understanding of the Trinity that stands the test of time. Because of the Trinity love is eternal and we can hope to live ultimately in a world of perfect love. "The grace of the Lord Jesus Christ, and the love of God, and the fellowship of the Holy Spirit be with you all" (2 Cor 13:13).

Scripture

Scripture is to be relied on as a source for truth as well as for understanding moral good. Developing a robust doctrine of Scripture requires careful attention; wrong views about Scripture lead to wrong conclusions about its applicability to growing in godliness. Three major emphases about the nature Scripture (the sixty-six books of the canon) are especially to be studied and grasped.

Its necessity. "Jesus spoke to them, 'Isn't this the reason why you're mistaken: you don't know the Scriptures or the power of God?'" (Mark 12:24). Certainly, it's possible to know something about the existence of God by observing the world and by considering conscience, as Paul made clear in Romans 1. Yet these are insufficient. The Bible is required for knowing the gospel and for knowing God's will. The journey to Christlikeness is stillborn without Scripture.

Its authority. Because Scripture is indeed the Word of God (in the words of men), it has authority over us. "All Scripture is inspired by God and is profitable for teaching for rebuilding, for correcting, for training in righteousness" (2 Tim 3: 16). The internal statements of Scripture about itself lead us to conclude that whatever Scripture teaches is to be believed and obeyed.

Its interpretation. Like every other written document, the words of the Bible must be interpreted (Luke 24:45). This means explaining the message of a passage as it was meant to be understood in its original setting but then to discover its significance in our contemporary setting. On one hand, the Bible's essential teachings can be understood by all who read it seeking God's help and committed to following its teachings. On the other hand, the Spirit of God is necessary to illumine the minds and hearts of believers to proper interpretation.

Creation and Mankind

"The earth and everything in it, the world and its inhabitants, belong to the Lord" (Ps 24:1). As noted in the worldview discussion, what it means to be human must be understood if we are to grow toward Christlikeness. Here we focus on certain aspects of creation that are good; later we will consider the issue of sin and evil.

Because of God's "omnis," he does whatever it pleases him to do. This includes his original creative acts, his sustaining of the universe, and his intervention in the natural order ("the laws of nature"); thus, divine miracles are possible at any time (Acts 2:22). God's creation includes *supernatural beings* serving him in a variety of ways (collectively called angels).

The first chapter of the Bible affirms that mankind was created in *God's image* (Gen. 1:26). This is never defined, but much of the discussion has focused on the following: *personality* (intellect and affections); *morality* (the ability to choose what is right); *spirituality* (the ability to relate to other persons); and (4) *representation* (serving as God's emissaries to the rest of the created order). Further, we recognize the *marriage relationship*, a binding agreement between one man and one woman to live together, maintain a home, share sexual intimacy, and usually to bear children. Jesus affirmed this view of marriage in Matthew 19:4–6, quoting from Genesis 2.

Sin

"Sin" has been banished from public conversation. We speak about mistakes or failings; we recognize a few scandalous crimes as evil (terrorism or child molestation or sex trafficking), but we don't speak of sin anymore. Yet the Bible assumes sin on virtually every page. We need to wrestle with the nature of human sin. Are we essentially good people, with sin as an occasional aberration? Or are we now fallen and sinners by birth, prone toward evil?

Original sin refers to the distortion and damage that our first parents passed on to all their descendants, so that everyone is born in a sinful condition. "Therefore, just as sin entered the world through one man, and death through sin, in this way death spread to all people, because all sinned" (Rom 5:12).

Depravity refers to the tendency toward sinning. All humans are inclined away from loving God and toward self-centeredness. Depravity does not mean that we are as evil as we can possibly be but rather that we are stained by evil through and through. "All of us have become like something unclean, and all our righteous acts are like a polluted garment; all of us wither like a leaf, and our iniquities carry us away like the wind" (Isa 64:6).

The origin of sin and evil has been widely debated. What is clear is that the *devil and demons* are supernatural beings created good by God who fell into sin. They oppose God by tempting, accusing, and leading astray. "Your adversary the devil is prowling around like a roaring lion, looking for anyone he can devour" (1 Pet 5:8). Because God is holy and will not tolerate sin forever, he has designated *hell* as the final place and condition for evil spirits and evil human beings. "Then he [the King] will also say to those on the left, 'Depart from me, you who are cursed, into the eternal fire prepared for the devil and his angels!'" (Matt 25:41).

Jesus Christ

Study of the Lord Jesus Christ usually follows two broad categories: the person of Christ (who he is) and the work of Christ (what he has done). As to his person, the biblical teaching is that Jesus is *fully God*, with all the attributes of deity: "We wait for the blessed hope, the appearing of the glory of our great

God and Savior, Jesus Christ" (Titus 2:13). He is God the Son or Son of God. Equally, however, Jesus is *fully human*, with all the attributes of humanity, sin only excluded. Thus, his birth to a woman (yes, a virgin, Luke 1:34–35); his normal development (Luke 2:52); his ability to be tempted (Luke 4:1–13); his ability to suffer (Luke 22:39–46); and his death by violent means and burial (Luke 23:44–56) all point to his humanity.

As early generations of Christians wrestled with the serious matter of how the humanity and deity of Christ relate, one of the first widely accepted statements was the Apostles' Creed, which began: "I believe in God the Father Almighty, Maker of heaven and earth, and in Jesus Christ his only Son our Lord, who was conceived by the Holy Ghost, born of the Virgin Mary." Later, more complete statements came from the Council of Nicaea (AD 325) and the Council of Constantinople (AD 381), in which consensus emerged. Confessing Christians affirm that Jesus Christ has *two natures (human and divine) but is only one person.*

Christ's work may be summarized in a single word: *atonement*. The term refers to bringing alienated parties together by making amends for what caused the separation. In his suffering and death Jesus fully paid the penalty for our sins, dying as the only atoning sacrifice for sinners, a substitute in our place. "He [God] made the one who did not know sin to be sin for us, so that in him we might become the righteousness of God" (2 Cor 5:21). Jesus's bodily resurrection proves that his death was sufficient; he is now the exalted Lord of all: "After making purification for sins, he sat down at the right hand of the Majesty on high" (Heb 1:3).

Salvation

In Scripture "salvation" is the broadest term used for the rescue of sinners from death to eternal life with God. This may be spoken of as "salvation in three tenses." God *has saved* the sinner from the penalty of sin at conversion; he *is saving* the sinner from the power of sin throughout life; and he *will save* the sinner from the presence of sin at the resurrection. Theologians and Scripture use multiple concepts to show what salvation includes. The following are among the most significant.

Predestination. This issue has been the source of great debate, yet the Bible teaches that "those he [God] foreknew he also predestined to be conformed to the image of his Son" (Rom 8:29). The verb translated "predestine" occurs six times in the New Testament: Acts 4:28; Romans 8:29–30; 1 Corinthians 2:7; Ephesians 1:5, 11. Some devout Christians interpret these passages to mean that God's omniscience is at work in predestination (he saw ahead of time those who would choose Christ). Other devout believers understand the passages to teach that because of human depravity, none would ever believe in Christ unless God first chose them to receive salvation. In any case, "the chosen people" is a noteworthy biblical concept.

Regeneration. Being "born again" refers to God's making a person alive spiritually, a supernatural work of the Spirit in which sinners are given new life. Jesus's encounter with Nicodemus in John 3:1–8 is the classic text (see also 1 Cor 5:17 and Titus 3:5).

Repentance and faith. Those who receive salvation first turn away from sin (repentance) and simultaneously turn to Christ as Savior (faith). Thus, Paul complimented the Thessalonian believers who "turned to God from idols" (1 Thess 1:9). Trusting in Jesus Christ alone—specifically the value of his atoning death—is the heart of this belief. Such belief is much more than assent (believing that certain facts are true) or temporal faith (believing that God will take care of a time-bound situation). The New Testament writers loved to quote Genesis 15:6 to show that salvation by faith has always been God's plan: "Abraham believed the LORD, and he credited it to him as righteousness" (see Rom 4:3, 9, 22; Gal 3:6; Jas 2:23).

Justification. Justification is God's judicial declaration that a sinner who believes in Christ is counted righteous instead of guilty before him because of Jesus's death on his or her behalf. Christ's righteousness is credited to the sinner, just as God counted our sins to Jesus on the cross. "Justification by faith alone" was the truth of the gospel that the Reformers of the sixteenth century (such as Martin Luther and John Calvin) brilliantly recovered. "Therefore, since we have been declared righteous by faith, we have peace with God through our Lord Jesus Christ" (Rom 5:1).

Adoption. The heavenly Father grants family status and benefits (such as access to God and a spiritual inheritance) to all believers. "Because you are sons, God sent the Spirit of his Son into our hearts, crying, "*Abba*, Father!" So you are no longer a slave but a son, and if you are a son, then God has made you an heir" (Gal 4:6–7).

The Church

For many followers of Jesus, participation in a local congregation has become optional. Biblically, however, there is no such thing as a follower of Christ not actively involved in the life of a congregation. In other words, discipleship—living the Christian life well and growing toward Christlikeness—works only in the context of participating in the body of Christ.

Jesus gave commands concerning rituals all his followers are to practice: *baptism* (an initiation ceremony) and *the Lord's Supper* (or Communion or the Eucharist, an ongoing-fellowship ceremony), noted in Matthew 28:19–20 and Luke 22:19. These are community events that are not to be carried out individualistically. *Gifts of the Spirit* have been poured out on persons not for their benefit but so that others will benefit: "Just as each one has received a gift, use it to serve others, as good stewards of the varied grace of God. If anyone speaks, let it be as one who speaks

God's words; if anyone serves, let it be from the strength God provides, so that God may be glorified through Jesus Christ in everything" (1 Pet 4:10–11). The responsibility for *evangelism and missions* is best fulfilled by local congregations, as the book of Acts demonstrates. Further, it must be noted that the *fruit of the Spirit* (Gal 5:22–23) occurs only in relationship with other people.

Last Things

Study of Christ's return and events surrounding it can generate more heat than light. The cause of Christ has suffered embarrassment from overzealous prophets and "date setters." Framers of the Apostles' Creed were content with the following statements about the last things: "He [Christ] will come to judge the living and the dead. . . . I believe in . . . the resurrection of the body and the life everlasting." The overall impact of the biblical teaching is that we are responsible to live now with the awareness that our earthly journey is preparation for eternity.

Certain truths concerning the last things are beyond dispute:

The second coming of Christ. The resurrected, exalted Jesus will personally, visibly, bodily, and victoriously return to earth as King of kings and Lord of lords (Acts 1:11).

The final judgment. Through Jesus Christ, God will issue the final verdict on all human beings, with one of two eternal destinies: eternal joy in God's presence or eternal misery cast away from all hope of God and good (1 Chr 16:31–33).

The new heavens and the new earth. "For I will create a new heaven and a new earth; the past events will not be remembered or come to mind" (Isa 65:17). "But based on his promise, we wait for new heavens and a new earth, where righteousness dwells" (2 Pet 3:13).

Other biblical teachings about the end times have been vigorously disputed:

The nature of the rapture. First Thessalonians 4:16–17 teaches that the dead in Christ will rise first at his coming; then those alive will be caught up to meet him in the air. (The term "rapture" is based on the Latin rendering of "caught up.") The timing of this event and whether it is to be understood as secret or public are hotly contested.

The nature of the tribulation. How are we to understand the meaning of texts such as Matthew 24:21–22? Can a specific timeline for the final affliction brought against God's people be developed? How do the "seals" and "trumpets" and "bowls" of Revelation fit together?

The nature of the millennium. Revelation 20 speaks of a 1000-year period in which martyrs come to life and reign on the earth with Christ. How literally should this be understood? Is this event before or after the second coming? How does this teaching relate to the teaching that believers have already been raised spiritually and seated in the heavens with Christ (Eph 2:6)?

Reflective Questions

- Has theology been a dirty word for you or something you have avoided? Why?
- Why is it so important for you to grasp of what the Bible teaches about essential topics?
- What steps can you take to become a more intentional theologian?

SCRIPTURE (BREAKFAST WITH THE FATHER)

Scripture is the Word of God in the words of men. It is the bread the heavenly Father has provided for his people's benefit. Jesus himself affirmed this in his encounter with the tempter in the wilderness (Matt 4:4). The "breakfast menu items" we have looked at so far—doxology, worldview, and theology—all depend directly on Scripture in one way or another. Thus, the reality that all things exist for God's glory is known only through Scripture. The chapter on worldview emphasized that the Bible is a necessary source for truth and for morality. Our outline of theology was based on asking, What does the whole Bible teach us today about any given topic?

If we are to encounter Scripture well, three matters are essential. First is grasping the "big story" of Scripture. Second is learning something about the disciplined study of Scripture. Third is sacred reading, the contemplative experience of seeking to be shaped by the Word.

The Big Story of the Bible

When I was a little boy, Mother read to me incessantly from a beloved Bible storybook, The Child's Story Bible (by Catherine Vos, first published in 1935 and still in print). I learned the narratives by heart, from Adam and Eve, to the exodus, to David, to Elijah and Ahab, to Jesus and the wedding at Cana (my favorite), to Paul and Silas in prison. Without formal instruction, I developed a decent sense of the overall story that the Bible tells.

In today's culture, knowing someone's personal narrative—their life story so far—is increasingly prized. Yet many people seem to be at sea when it comes to identifying any larger story providing them with a life context and meaning, sometimes called a metanarrative. Thus, one of the challenges facing Americans these days is that we've lost our sense of the American story and how we each belong to it. This factor contributes to the increased fracturing of our society. We don't share the same story about our country.

After four decades of teaching college and seminary students, I've seen a parallel decline in understanding of biblical story, the great storyline that explains the pattern of truth Scripture presents. Certainly my students have heard of Noah and Ruth and Esther and Jesus on the cross. But they haven't connected the dots. To remedy this problem, several Christian thinkers and writers have recently begun telling Bible's story around four concepts or movements: creation, fall, redemption, and restoration.

- *Creation.* God's creation was 100 percent good. Earth was filled with peace (*shalom*). Everything necessary for human flourishing and for glorifying God perfectly was in place.
- *Fall.* Our first parents rejected God, and all their descendants became a race of rebels. This rebellion resulted in physical and spiritual death for all humankind.
- *Redemption.* God initiated his plan for saving the world and rescuing fallen sinners. God became man, and the pinnacle for redemption was Jesus's death and resurrection.
- *Restoration.* God has promised to renew the world. Christ will return to judge sin and evil, and he will usher in an eternity of righteousness and perfect peace (*shalom*).

My book, The Illustrated Guide to Biblical History (2003), displays the story of the Bible in a slightly different way. I show that we can think of six great "chapters" in the story, all of which develop the Bible's central teaching: "The Lord God through his Christ is graciously building a kingdom of redeemed people for their joy and for his own glory" (p. 3).

Prologue: The need for redemption (Genesis 1–11)

- Creation and fall
- Flood and Babel
- Humanity is a race of rebels against God

1. **God builds his nation: Israel chosen as God's people** (Gen 12–1 Kgs 11; 2000–931 BC)

   - Call of Abraham: *covenant promising worldwide blessing* (Gen 12)
   - Exodus (redemption from slavery)
   - Law and land: *temporary Mosaic covenant of the law* (Exod 20; see Heb 8:13)
   - Kingship and temple: *covenant promising eternal son of David* (2 Sam 7)

2. **God educates his nation: Rebellious Israel punished** (1 Kgs 11–2 Kgs 25, Isaiah, Wisdom books; 931–586 BC)

   - Nation divided
   - Northern Kingdom (Israel) conquered by Assyria
   - Southern Kingdom (Judah) conquered by Babylon and temple destroyed

3. **God keeps a faithful remnant: Preparation for the coming Messiah** (Ezra–Esther; many prophets; 586–6 BC)

   - Return from 70-year captivity
   - Law and land reestablished
   - Second temple built

- The long wait predicted: Babylon, Persia, Greece, and Rome (Dan 2)

  New covenant predicted, promising forgiveness and transformed life (Jeremiah 31)

4. **God purchases redemption and begins the kingdom: Jesus the Messiah** (four Gospels; 6 BC–AD 30)

   - Incarnation and virgin birth of Jesus
   - Life and ministry of Jesus
   - Crucifixion, resurrection, and exaltation of Jesus

   New covenant established (Luke 22:20)

5. **God spreads the kingdom through the church: the current age** (Acts and the Epistles; AD 30–?)

   - Beginning of the church in Jerusalem: The new age of the Spirit
   - Expansion of the church: Jews and Gentiles as one body of Christ
   - Christian history: temple and Israelite nation obsolete

6. **God consummates his kingdom: Redemption completed** (book of Revelation; AD ??)

   - Satanic rage against God's people permitted
   - God's wrath against Satan and evil poured out
   - The glorious return of Christ and final judgment

Epilogue: New heavens and new earth (Rev 21—22)

Disciplined Study of the Bible

One of the best recent guides for helping us interpret and apply the message of Scripture—whether an entire Bible book or just a few verses—is Gordon Fee and Douglas Stuart's How to Read the Bible for All Its Worth: A Guide to Understanding the Bible. They remind us that the first major task of Scripture study is to seek to understand what the text meant in its original setting (exegesis). Only then can we approach the second task: seeking to understand the significance of the text, what it means for our lives today (hermeneutics). Thus, a text cannot mean today what it could not have meant in its original setting.

Context. The Bible is to be studied like any other literary work. It has words and sentences and paragraphs that a human author (inspired by God, to be sure) wrote down. Thus, with an excellent translation in hand, when we seek to understand what the text meant "back in the day," we will ask questions such as these: Who was the human author? What was the original audience? When was it written? Where was it written? Did the author say why it was written? If this sounds a bit like asking the kinds of questions your high school literature teacher taught you to ask as you approached a short story or an essay or a biography, you are right.

Understanding the context of a passage also includes coming to good conclusions about its literary form. Thus, the Old Testament historical books (and the Gospels and Acts) are mainly historical narrative, meant to be understood as reliable accounts. But then many other passages must be understood as laws (commands to be obeyed). Other passages are prophecies (with predictions as well as exhortations). Then the Psalms and parts of other books are poetry (with much symbolic language). Further, there is wisdom material (principles for living well). Not to be forgotten are fictional elements, stories that were never understood as literally happening (such as the parables of Jesus). Only when we have wrestled through such matters, for example, recognizing the difference between biblical commands and wisdom precepts, will we be on the right road to proper interpretation.

Content. Next, we may study the meaning of individual terms (word studies) and look at the grammatical structure of a passage. We look at how the concepts in the passage are used elsewhere in the Bible (cross references) or how a New Testament author quoted or referred to an Old Testament text. Bible dictionaries and commentaries are valuable resources here. The notes in a reliable study Bible are treasure troves; for example, those based on the Christian Standard Bible, the English Standard Version, and the New International Version are standouts.

In seeking to understand what a passage meant originally, we also ask "belief and behavior" questions. Thus, assuming we have come to terms with the major topics of theology (as noted in the previous chapter), we ask such questions as these:

- What does the passage teach about God (his person or his works)?
- What does the passage teach about humanity (as created or as fallen into sin)?
- What does the passage teach about Jesus Christ (his person or his work)?
- What does the passage teach about salvation?
- What does the passage teach about the church (our life in community)?

Once these questions are answered, other questions the passage raises inevitably come up. There is no set list of content questions to be raised. Further, for most passages we can ask questions about implications for our behavior:

- What does the passage imply about good and evil, right and wrong?
- What does the passage imply about justice, for persons or for society?
- What does the passage imply about personal morality?
- What does the passage imply about the great commandments: loving God with all one's being and loving one's neighbors as oneself?
- What does the passage imply about living in the kingdom of God?

Concerns. At last we come to terms with the significance of the text for today. If the Bible is the Word of God in the words of men, then it is relevant. We do not have to make it relevant; we only have to discover the relevance of the text for today. Sometimes the contemporary meaning is closely related to the original meaning, such Paul's brilliant discussion of the humiliation and exaltation of Jesus Christ in Philippians 2. On the other hand, sometimes relevance is quite indirect, such as the regulations concerning cleansing from skin diseases in Leviticus 14.

This is the time to ask, "So what?" of the passage. What difference should this passage make to my life here and now? For example, is God's glory displayed in a way that I can appreciate and must respond to? Are there lessons for life that encourage or warn me? Is the Spirit of God at work in my life internally as I study the text, challenging me to change something in my beliefs or behavior? How might the Lord mean for me to apply this text to a specific situation I am facing. In other words, now that I have studied the context and the content, now what? When I remember that the Word of God is an agent of change as I grow in godliness, I cannot be content with mere exegesis. I will recognize the urgency of applying the text to my life.

Sacred Reading of the Bible

For the past two hundred years or so, systematic study was thought of as the primary—if not the only—goal in approaching Scripture. For many, however, this meant that the Bible became dry and dusty. There was often little life change. To be sure, many a pious Christian did manage to read Scripture devotionally. Yet in the twentieth century an ancient approach to Scripture was recovered, emphasizing meditation and contemplation on Scripture as a means of communion with God. Benedict of Nursia (AD 480–547), founder of the Benedictine order of monks, introduced "sacred reading" (in Latin, lectio divina) into daily practice in his monastic communities. Later, the four movements of sacred reading were crystalized. These four movements have been compared to a feast on the Word: taking a bite (lectio, or reading); chewing on it (meditatio, or meditation); savoring it (oratio, or praying it back to God); and then making it part of one's life (contemplatio, or contemplation). The mystic Christian John of the Cross (AD 1542–91) summarized this way: "Seek in reading and you will find in meditation; knock in prayer and it will be opened to you in contemplation."

Sacred reading may be learned, practiced, and enjoyed by those who are neither monks nor Roman Catholics. Kenneth Boa's work, Conformed to His Image, sketched a way for all followers of Jesus to practice the movements involved in sacred reading (pp. 174–85).

Read. This involves the quiet, slow preparation of stilling oneself in God's presence before beginning. It includes inviting the Spirit of God to speak through the process. As Paul wrote to the Corinthians: "But as it is written, 'What no eye has seen, no ear has heard, and no human heart has conceived—God has prepared these things for those who love him.' Now God has revealed these things to us by the Spirit, since the Spirit searches everything, even the depths of God." (1 Cor 2:9–10). Then comes the process of reading a brief passage (usually not more than two or three verses) slowly, orally, gradually, and attentively. The text is read several times, perhaps with a slightly different emphasis on various parts of the text. For example, in John 3:16, the following words or phrases could be the focus:

- For **God** loved the world in this way: He gave His One and Only Son . . .
- For God **loved** the world in this way: He gave His One and Only Son . . .
- For God loved **the world** in this way: He gave His One and Only Son . . .
- For God loved the world **in this way**: He gave His One and Only Son . . .
- For God loved the world in this way: **He gave** His One and Only Son . . .
- For God loved the world in this way: He gave **His One and Only Son** . . .

Meditate. The focus is on listening to the message the Spirit might want to convey through the passage. It's like soaking in a moving stream, seeking what the Lord is saying intuitively or subjectively through the text. We ponder the text, not with our own pre-determined understanding but to consider it from various angles. This is not the time for analysis but for keeping one's heart open. For example, consider Jesus's words in John 14:27: "Peace I leave with you. My peace I give to you." A disciplined, analytical approach will focus on the original context (Jesus's last supper), why Jesus said this (the disciples' fear), or even theological investigation (the high cost that Jesus paid in providing peace). In meditation on this text, I seek to enter the peace of Jesus, seeking peace through communion with God.

Pray. This movement involves praying Scripture back to God. We often think of Scripture as God's Word to us and prayer as our words to God. But what if we first read and meditate on the Word and then have a conversation with God about what we have read? What if we remain in God's presence and expect a two-way conversation, whether in words that can be verbalized or simply by impressions? If the Word of God is really a "lamp for my feet and a light for my path," then we will treasure Scripture even more highly as we recognize its illuminating power in our lives. Will we praise God or thank him or ask him for divine help in response to our reading and meditation? Sometimes praying Scripture is sweet and comforting; sometimes it involves pain and confession; sometimes it involves adoration and praise. But it cannot be done in a hurry or demanding certain outcomes.

Contemplate. In this sense, contemplation is understood as silence in God's presence. It is being attentive to the presence of God in and through the Word of God. This is a matter of remaining wordless, seeking the occasion to express love for God in one's inner person because of the privilege of reading, meditating, and praying the Word. Whether he speaks directly or not, such contemplation is an active expression of commitment and love for him. Contemplation is a discipline that takes time to develop. It doesn't come naturally, because it is the work of God in our hearts. Yet it is worth it to give up on analysis and learn to be drawn ever more deeply into the depths of God's love.

Reflective Questions: Scripture

- How would you articulate the grand story of the Bible to an interested friend?
- How important is it for you to learn to carry out disciplined Scripture study?
- How willing are you to learn to approach Scripture through sacred reading?

PART 2

LUNCH WITH THE SPIRIT OR SPRITUAL FORMATION

Growing in godliness continues as we experience the Holy Spirit's presence and activity in our lives. The "lunch focus" is on those parts of growing in godliness that recognize the Spirit as giving us the power to be holy as well as to do the works we are called to fulfill. The menu includes the following.

Spiritual power. The ascended Jesus gave his people the gift of the Spirit on Pentecost. The Spirit in turn gives spiritual gifts to individual believers so that we build up other believers. Paul's teaching on spiritual gifts is the most extensive in Scripture. The charismatic movement has exploded in the past century as evidence that spiritual gifts are still active.

Spiritual fruit. The Bible contains many lists of desirable character qualities or virtues, the fruit of the Spirit, which are evidence of the Spirit's work in a person. Classically, the four cardinal virtues are prudence, justice, temperance, and fortitude. The three theological virtues are faith, hope, and love. These are essential for a life of flourishing.

Spiritual health. Even long-term believers may drift into unhealthy life patterns. External factors—the world—produce many allures. Yet internal factors—the flesh—often fail us. Following biblical prescriptions for spiritual health can help cure "dis-ease."

Spiritual discipline. The classic spiritual disciplines are instruments the Spirit often uses to move us toward spiritual maturity. We begin with disciplines of denial; we continue with exercises designed to open our hearts to God personally; we also choose disciplines that necessarily mean we will engage others, such as worship and service.

SPIRITUAL POWER
(LUNCH WITH THE SPIRIT)

As we transition from thinking about biblical formation to spiritual formation, our focus will be on the ways the Holy Spirit works in us as followers of Jesus. Several items are on our "lunch menu," and an important place to begin is to consider the power of the Spirit in the life of believers.

When the risen Jesus was about to ascend to the Father, he assured the apostles, "You will receive power when the Holy Spirit has come on you" (Acts 1:8). His promise began to be fulfilled a few days later, on Pentecost. These followers of Jesus certainly could not have grasped fully what the power of the Spirit would be like in their lives, yet they should have had some clues. First, there was Jesus's own ministry in the power of the Spirit (Luke 4:14). He was explicit that his miracle-working ministry was carried out by the Spirit (Matt 12:28).

Second, there were stories about heroes of old whom the Spirit empowered to do the works of God.

Thus, Samson the judge (hardly a righteous leader) did mighty deeds by the Spirit's power (Judg 14:10; 15:14). King Saul was empowered by the Spirit temporarily (1 Sam 10:10; 16:14). Ezekiel the prophet was empowered by the Spirit to carry out a difficult ministry (Ezek 2:1–3). The biblical evidence is that, before Pentecost, the power of the Spirit came temporarily on only a few persons. The Book of Acts shows how dramatically this changed.

The Spirit's Power in Acts

When the Spirit was poured out powerfully on 120 disciples of Jesus on the day of Pentecost, Peter preached that this began to fulfill the prophecy of Joel 2:28–32. Gloriously, the Spirit was poured out not on just a select few but on all God's people (Acts 2:17–18), not just on men but also women). And as far as the evidence in the text of Scripture goes, no woman in the Old Testament was noted as empowered by the Spirit. The Spirit was poured out not temporarily but as the enduring gift of the risen Christ to his people, referred to as being baptized with the Spirit (Mark 1:8; Acts 1:5). Thus, Paul reminded the believers in Rome that the permanent indwelling presence of the Spirit was one mark of true believers: "If anyone does not have the Spirit of Christ, he does not belong to him" (Rom 8:9). The Spirit himself was the gift Jesus promised to send (John 14:16, 26). There could be no greater gift to his people than his own presence in and with them.

The Spirit's power was in evidence in many ways in Acts. The Spirit empowered the disciples' preaching, so that many were converted to the faith (Acts 2:40–41; 4:31; 8:29–40). The Spirit produced miracles of healing, continuing the pattern of Jesus's miracles (Acts 3:6–8; 9:40; 14:10). The Spirit empowered disciples to speak in languages they had never studied or learned (Acts 2:4; 10:44–46; 19:6). Paul later explained the Spirit's presence as manifested through a variety of gifts, or charismata (Rom 12:6; 1 Cor 12:4).

The Spirit's Gifts in Paul's Letters

The two great passages in Paul dealing with spiritual gifts are Romans 12 and 1 Corinthians 12–14. Certain facts about spiritual gifts are abundantly clear.

- Each believer has at least one gift (1 Cor 12:7).
- Spiritual gifts are to be used to build up other believers (Rom 12:6–7; 1 Cor 12:7).
- There is no "set list" of spiritual gifts, for the Romans and 1 Corinthians lists are different.
- The use of spiritual gifts does not prove spiritual maturity or godliness (1 Cor 1:7; 3:1; 13:2).
- Not all believers have (or should seek) the spiritual gift of tongues (1 Cor 12:30).

- The gift of prophecy is much more important than the gift of tongues (1 Cor 14:1–3).
- In worship, the gift of tongues is prohibited unless there is interpretation (1 Cor 14:27–28).
- Only when spiritual gifts are motivated by love are they worth anything (1 Cor 13:2–3).

So then, if you are reading this as a follower of Jesus Christ, you have at least one spiritual gift. This gift was given to you when you were born again, analogous to the natural talents you received when you were born into this world. Just as you had nothing to do with which talents you were born with (analytical skill, athleticism, musicality), so you had nothing to do with which spiritual gifts you received. They are a matter of God's grace extended to you. (The New Testament word for grace is charis; the term for spiritual gift is charisma; plural is charismata.)

Further, it's your responsibility, as a member of Christ's community, to use your gifts to encourage and build up other believers. Some gifts seem to arrive fully developed, such as speaking in tongues or gifts of healing; others—like talents—thrive best when they are cultivated, such as administration. At the same time, just because you have enjoyed success in using spiritual gifts is no reason to be boastful or proud. It wasn't your doing that you were so gifted. Further, as Jesus pronounced in the Sermon on the Mount, some who exercised gifts of prophecy or miracle working or success in exorcism were never truly Jesus's disciples (Matt 7:21–23). As we'll see in the next chapter, the fruit of the Spirit rather than the gifts of the Spirit is evidence of growth in Christlikeness.

Paul's two lists of spiritual gifts were not meant to be comprehensive but rather are representative. Just as it would be difficult to come up with a comprehensive list of natural talents, so there is no benefit it seeking to compile a complete list of spiritual gifts. A few notes about each gift Paul listed, however, may to be beneficial.

Prophecy (Rom 12:6; 1 Cor 12:10, 28). Speaking what God has brought to mind about a particular situation; "forth-telling" rather than foretelling; perhaps closely related to the gift of preaching; must be evaluated by mature leaders (1 Cor 14:29–31; 1 Thess 5:19–21).

Service (Rom 12:7). Ministry; assistance; related to the noun translated deacon; providing whatever help is needed; a special ability for those so gifted, yet every believer is entrusted with the work of the ministry (Eph 4:12).

Teaching (Rom 12:7; 1 Cor 12:28). Ability to explain the meaning of a biblical passage or theme so that other believers will understand and apply biblical truth to life; closely related to those who are pastors or shepherds in congregations (Eph 4:12).

Exhorting (Rom 12:8). Encouraging or comforting others; may include challenging or counseling;

closely related to the title "Counselor" that Jesus gave to the Spirit (John 15:26; 16:7–8).

Giving (Rom 12:8). Having the ability and desire to help others financially "above and beyond," including individuals or the whole congregation; yet every believer is called on to give sacrificially (2 Cor. 9:6-15).

Leading (Rom 12:8). Literally "standing over" or "standing before"; having authority over; both a calling and a gift; closely related to those who are overseers (Greek episkopoi, traditionally "bishops," 1 Tim 3:1–7).

Showing mercy (Rom 12:8). Expressing kindness and assistance readily to those who are hurting, both physically and spiritually; yet all believers are to express mercy: "Blessed are the merciful, for they will be shown mercy" (Matt 5:7).

Message of wisdom and message of knowledge (1 Cor 12:8). Phrases found here only in the New Testament; ability to share insights with others concerning a wise course of action for a situation or concerning facts important for reaching good decisions.

Faith (1 Cor 12:9). Not saving faith (which all followers of Jesus express) but ready ability to trust God in situations of urgent need when others are doubtful; the "mustard seed faith" that Jesus praised (Matt 17:20).

Gifts of healing (1 Cor 12:9, 28). Literally "gifts of healings," suggesting that God uses others as his agents of healing in a variety of ways; connected closely to prayer and the anointing of the sick by the elders of a congregation (Jas 5:14–15).

Performing of miracles (1 Cor 12:9, 28). Literally "working of power"; continuing the miracle ministry of Jesus as evidence of the presence of the kingdom of God (Matt 12:28); may include exorcisms, that is, casting out evil spirits.

Distinguishing between spirits (1 Cor 12:10). Supernatural ability to discern whether those claiming to speak by the Spirit are telling the truth or are motivated by self or by evil spirits, perhaps even self-deceived (1 Thess 5:20–21; 1 John 4:1–6).

Different kinds of tongues (1 Cor 12:10, 28). Supernatural ability enabling some to speak instantly in earthly or ecstatic languages one never learned; a kind of prayer (1 Cor 13:1; 14:14); different than the tongues on Pentecost, which were understood by hearers; these tongues were not understood by the speaker (Acts 2:11; 1 Cor 14:9–13).

Interpretation of tongues (1 Cor 12:10, 30). Supernatural ability enabling some to translate into intelligent speech what another has spoken in tongues; tongues plus interpretation is equivalent to prophecy (1 Cor 14:5); in public worship, tongues if present must be interpreted or else the one so speaking must keep silent (1 Cor 14:29).

Helping (1 Cor 12:28). Ability to aid as needed; a term found here only in the New Testament; a near synonym for the noun translated "service" in Romans 12:7; likely related to those who were deacons (ministers or servants).

Administrating (1 Cor 12:28). Related closely to the term for a ship's captain or navigator; a term found here only in the New Testament; a near synonym for the noun translated "leading" in Romans 12:8; likely related to those who were elders or overseers.

This is quite a list! The Spirit has surely provided all the gifts required so that the Lord's people are equipped "for the work of the ministry, to build up the body of Christ, until we all reach unity in the faith and in the knowledge of God's Son growing into maturity with a stature measured by Christ's fullness" (Eph 4:12–13). What the apostle Paul has written here is the theme of this book: feast with the Trinity and become mature and Christlike.

The Spirit and the Charismatic Movement

For the past hundred years or so, one growing branch of Christianity has emphasized spiritual gifts more effectively than the three historic branches of the faith, whether Protestant, Roman Catholic, or Orthodox. The charismatic movement—an umbrella term I am using to include both the rise of Pentecostalism (beginning early in the twentieth century) as well as the rise of the charismatic movement among major denominations (beginning in the 1960s)—has spread in some parts of the world so that it has become the major expression of Christianity. Many observers now consider it to have become the fourth branch of Christianity. I indicated in the introduction to this book my own personal three-year charismatic phase.

In the paragraphs that follow, I offer personal observations, both by study and by experience, of the charismatic movement.

The most obvious strength of the charismatic movement has been a strong belief that all the spiritual gifts mentioned in the New Testament are available to today's Christians after they have experienced a powerful personal encounter with the Spirit. This empowerment typically has been called the baptism of the Spirit. Because of this expectancy, those involved in the movement have enjoyed great spiritual experiences. Both the more obviously miraculous gifts (prophecy, tongues, interpretation, and healings) and less spectacular gifts (teaching, leading, serving, showing mercy) have been in evidence. Simply put, because these believers have asked the Spirit to pour out his gifts, he has done so in ways that cannot be denied. The older branches of Christianity for far too long ignored or downplayed the gifts of the Spirit, consigning them to the first century or else emphasizing only the less spectacular gifts. After the rise of Pentecostal denominations in the first part of the twentieth century (such as the Assemblies of God and the Church of God in Christ), many in the other three older branches realized their lack. They began seeking out the exercise of spiritual gifts after an empowering encounter with the Spirit.

A second major strength of the charismatic movement has been expressive worship characterized by spontaneity. Lively music, hands raised, operation of gifts of the Spirit, and many praying aloud collectively have been hallmarks of charismatic gatherings. These provide a remarkable contrast with what has often appeared to be a dry or boring approach to public worship in traditional denominations. It was charismatic worship that attracted me to the movement. When I learned to expect the Spirit to "show up" in worship and let go of my inherent desire for rational control, I began to worship much more freely and enjoyably than I had done in the past. Something wonderful happens when Christian worship engages both the affections (emotions, feelings, engaging the Spirit's presence) as well as the mind (thinking, engaging the Word preached).

Nevertheless, there are valid criticisms of the charismatic movement. First is the misguided insistence among early Pentecostal preachers and teachers that their experience of tongues was the same as that recorded in Acts 2 (which involved speaking in known languages). Because these teachers paid more attention to Acts than to 1 Corinthians, they made the mistake of arguing that the baptism of the Spirit was a post-conversion experience required for spiritual power. Further, they claimed that speaking in tongues was the only acceptable evidence that one had been empowered by the Spirit. Yet Paul made it abundantly clear that with Christian conversion came the baptism of the Spirit (1 Cor 12:13). Further, the apostle's rhetorical question in 1 Corinthians 12:30 shows that not all believers are supposed to speak in tongues. Paul considered tongues a less-important spiritual gift (1 Cor. 14:19). At the same time, multiplied thousands of believers have experienced tongues along the lines of a private prayer language (1 Cor 14:14–18). I look back fondly on the day in 1974 when I experienced speaking in tongues as a prayer language.

Second, because the charismatic movement rightly recovered the gifts of the Spirit, sometimes the gift of the Spirit himself has been overlooked. Charismatic experiences were valued for their own sake rather than because they were a means toward spiritual growth. In recent decades the "prosperity gospel" has become an aberrant offshoot of the charismatic movement. These teachers claim that God always wants to give his people financial blessing and physical well-being. Thus, if someone has enough faith, God will deliver what they are entitled to: prosperity, health, and happiness. Other charismatic leaders, as well as those from traditional branches of Christianity, have noted with dismay that such health and wealth teaching is irresponsible and contrary to Scripture. It constitutes a form of idolatry. When persons seek the blessings of God more than God himself, something is seriously amiss.

A third criticism is that because of the emphasis on personal experience, careful biblical and theological thinking sometimes has been neglected by leaders in the charismatic movement. Traditional denominations have engaged in in-depth research and publication, perhaps to a fault. Yet it's essential for believers of all stripes seek to balance between being "Word centered" and "Spirit centered." Head and heart need not be separated. Or in terms of the present book, the path to Christlike maturity includes not only biblical formation (breakfast with the Father) but also spiritual formation (lunch with the Spirit).

As we have seen, the Spirit of God means to empower God's people. Jesus promised the power of the Spirit, and Acts shows how this happened historically. Paul pointed the way to an understanding of the gifts of the Spirit. And among today's Christians, we may seek wisdom regarding our personal involvement with charismatic believers.

Reflective Questions

- What evidence do you have that you possess the indwelling Spirit as a permanent gift?
- Have you identified your gifts from the Spirit? How are you using them to build up others?
- How do you evaluate today's charismatic movement?

SPIRITUAL FRUIT
(LUNCH WITH THE SPIRIT)

In his Upper Room Discourse Jesus broached several topics urgent for him to impart to the apostles before he was arrested. Among these was his extensive development of the analogy of the vine and the branches. Producing much fruit (that is, Christ-like character) goes hand in hand with being a genuine follower of Jesus. Jesus's Beatitudes in the Sermon on the Mount constitute a fantastic list of godly fruit (Matt 5:1–8). Yet solemnly he also warned in the same sermon many who exercised miraculous gifts were frauds (Matt 7:21–23). In a similar vein, Paul warned the Corinthian believers, who lacked no spiritual gift, that they were worldly and immature (1 Cor 1:7; 3:1). Thus, the active exercise of spiritual gifts is no evidence of growth in Christlikeness. Let's think together about the "menu item" of spiritual fruit.

Paul taught believers in Galatia, "But the fruit of the Spirit is love, joy, peace, patience, kindness, goodness, faithfulness, gentleness and self-control" (Gal 5:22–23). This was the apostle's development of the "much fruit" teaching of Jesus. For Paul, love was the principal fruit, with all the other qualities emanating from love (agape). Just as light passing through a prism is divided into its many color components, so love, passing through the circumstances of daily life, appears as whatever fruit of the Spirit is called for. Peter's similar list of Christian virtues culminated with love (2 Pet 1:5–7). Peter introduced his list with the notion that building such character is something for which believers must "make every effort" (1:5). Several virtue lists occur in the New Testament Epistles. Note the following.

Virtue Lists in the Epistles

- Character of Paul's ministry, 2 Corinthians 6:6–8
- Fruit of the Spirit, Galatians 5:22–23
- Qualities of the new life, Ephesians 4:32
- Fruit of the light, Ephesians 5:9
- Excellent things to dwell on, Philippians 4:8
- Qualities to put on, Colossians 3:12
- Qualities to model, 1 Timothy 4:12
- Things for the man of God to pursue, 1 Timothy 6:11
- Qualities to pursue along with others, 2 Timothy 2:22

- Character of Paul's ministry, 2 Timothy 3:10
- Wisdom from above, James 3:17
- Qualities believers are called to, 1 Peter 3:8
- Qualities that keep believers from being unfruitful, 2 Peter 1:5–7

Reading through the passages listed, much less studying them in depth, gives the impression that they have no discernible pattern. There was no set list of virtues or spiritual fruit. Thus, Christians through the centuries have often streamlined the biblical teaching regarding spiritual fruit—the Christ-like character traits worthy of diligent attention. The language of "put on" and "pursue" makes clear we are to strive toward these. At the same time, Jesus's teaching about remaining in the vine and Paul's use of "fruit of the Spirit" language emphasizes that only with the Spirit's help will our character become virtuous.

Character building is demanding because there are so many vices that we struggle against. Thus, the New Testament writers also often listed vices to beware of. As you look at the following lists, note that the biblical writers wrote with a healthy awareness of the perils we face because of the three enemies of the soul: the world, the flesh, and the devil.

Vice Lists

- Qualities that defile a person, Matthew 15:19

- Qualities coming from an evil heart, Mark 7:21–22
- What God delivers immoral persons over to, Romans 1:29–31
- Nighttime activities to avoid, Romans 13:13
- Behaviors in so-called believers that should cause a break in fellowship, 1 Corinthians 5:11
- Lifestyles not permitted in the kingdom, 1 Corinthians 6:9–10
- Activities requiring repentance, 2 Corinthians 12:20–21
- Works of the flesh, Galatians 5:19–21
- Qualities to be removed, Ephesians 4:31
- Qualities that should not be heard of among believers, Ephesians 5:3–5
- Qualities to put to death, Colossians 3:5, 8
- Those for whom the law is meant, 1 Timothy 1:9–10
- Last-days people to avoid, 2 Timothy 3:2–4
- The way believers used to be, Titus 3:3
- Qualities to get rid of, 1 Peter 2:1
- Behaviors of pagans, 1 Peter 4:3
- Reasons for which one may deservedly suffer, 1 Peter 4:15
- Actions that evil people refuse to repent of, Revelation 9:21

- Those to be cast into the lake of fire, Revelation 21:8
- Those prohibited from the new Jerusalem, Revelation 22:15

We stand today on the shoulders of Christians who have preceded us in thinking hard about Christian character. The church fathers of earlier centuries, reflecting both on Scripture and on pre-Christian philosophers, organized spiritual fruit into the "seven Christian virtues." They affirmed the four virtues advocated by pre-Christian philosophers, the four "cardinal virtues." To these were added three "theological virtues" that are possible only within a Christian context. When we move toward these ideals we are becoming more like God himself.

The Four Cardinal Virtues

Greek philosophers such as Plato and Aristotle articulated the moral fiber they believed was required for human flourishing (see Plato, The Republic; Aristotle, The Nicomachean Ethics). They were persuaded that four character traits formed the basis for all other virtues, which can and ought to be practiced by everyone (thus forming the basis for natural morality). For example, Plato narrated a discussion of the character of a good city where the following is agreed to: "Clearly, then, it will be wise, brave, temperate, and just" (Republic, 427e). Jewish scholars before Christ occasionally referred to these four virtues as a group (Wisdom of Solomon 8:7; 4 Maccabees 1:18–19), showing the influence of Greek thinking on these authors. The New Testament writers, however, show no awareness of the cardinal virtues as a group. Perhaps it was because pagan thinkers believed virtue could be achieved by human effort and did not require commitment to Christ and the gospel.

When Christian thinkers embraced these four character qualities as both desirable and compatible with the teaching of Scripture, they called them cardinal virtues. The term "cardinal" comes from the Latin cardo (hinge). They were cardinal because they formed the essential foundation for a virtuous life. Augustine wrote, "For these four virtues (would that all felt their influence in their minds as they have their names in their mouths!), I should have no hesitation in defining them: that temperance is love giving itself entirely to that which is loved; fortitude is love readily bearing all things for the sake of the loved object; justice is love serving only the loved object, and therefore ruling rightly; prudence is love distinguishing with sagacity between what hinders it and what helps it" (Of the Morals of the Catholic Church, xv). In the following discussion, the traditional English translation for these virtues has been followed.

Prudence (Greek phronesis). Practical wisdom; understanding; the ability to choose appropriate actions. Ancient philosophers as well as Christian theologian Thomas Aquinas regarded prudence as the charioteer of the virtues; that is, it drove the others. Thus, for example, persons will live with justice only if they have developed the habit of deciding the best action to take in response to life circumstances. Prudence is essentially the same as the practical wisdom (Hebrew hokmah) so highly commended in the Book of Proverbs.

The New Testament writers, however, rarely used *phronesis* (only in Luke 1:17; Eph 1:8). Instead, they used the term "wisdom" (Greek *sophia*), found more than fifty times. *Sophia* occurs in texts that refer to God's wisdom, which he may impart to humans. *Sophia,* however, sometimes refers to natural, worldly wisdom. In today's English, "prudence" has fallen out of use and now implies cautiousness in the sense of reluctance to take risks. Thus, translations such as "understanding" or "practical judgment" better convey the sense.

Justice (Greek dikaiosune). Fairness; upright behavior; right dealings with others. The Greeks understood justice as harmony between the different demands made within a person or within a society. Yet even many of the Greeks acknowledged that justice is received and understood by humans only by divine revelation: what is right and fair is morally good only because God has commanded it. (Alternatively, if what is morally right and fair has been commanded by God because it is already right and fair, then God appears to be simply one who passes on a morality higher than himself.)

A great deal of debate about the nature of justice has taken place: Is justice part of natural law? Is it a human creation? Is it something that must be mutually agreed to? Further, in today's cultural context questions of social justice and restorative (or retributive) justice are often on people's minds. One recurring thorny question is this: Who gets to define what "social justice" is and upon what grounds?

The New Testament uses dikaiosune more than ninety times and absolutely assumes that justice (traditionally translated "righteousness") has its source in God who is just. The apostles followed the Old Testament with its emphasis on the Lord as righteous. The Epistle to the Romans sets forth "the righteousness of God," particularly emphasizing that God gives righteousness to humans based on faith (Rom 1:17; 3:21–26). This theological understanding of righteousness as a gift from God was certainly not what the ancient Greeks had in mind. Yet dikaiosune in the sense of fair dealings with others and upright behavior is often commended in the New Testament (for example, Eph 6:14; Heb 12:11; 1 Pet 2:24).

Temperance (Greek sophrosune). Restraint; moderation; self-control in dealing with one's appetites. For the Greeks, this virtue referred to what a person voluntarily refrained from doing. Temperance meant keeping natural impulses in check. Thus, it included restraint from retaliation (through forgiveness and nonviolence); restraint from excess in food, drink, and sex (through self-control); and restraint from arrogance (through modesty and humility). As with prudence, the New Testament writers did not pick up the pre-Christian emphasis. Sophrosune is found only twice, where it carries the idea of "good sense" (Acts 26:25; 1 Tim 2:9, 15).

Temperance has been reduced in modern usage to mean abstinence from alcoholic drink, based on the "temperance movement" of the early 1800s that condemned alcoholic beverages and promoted total abstinence. The original meaning for the Greeks as well as the church fathers was much broader, and translations such as "moderation" or "self-control" now better convey the sense of this quality.

Fortitude (Greek andreia). Courage; endurance; bravery; the ability to confront pain, fear, and intimidation. For the ancient Greeks, fortitude meant controlling one's fears and at the same time curbing rash or reckless behavior. Fortitude has often been contrasted with "animal courage," which attacks out of pain or anger or instinct. Fortitude is courage as an intentional choice. Physical fortitude is courage in the face of bodily pain, hardship, or threat of death. Moral fortitude refers to courage in the face of popular opposition, shame, scandal, discouragement, or loss.

Fortitude is closely related to the Greek noun aner (male, man, husband) and therefore implied some traditional sense of manliness. The New Testament does not use the term at all. In one instance only, Paul used the related verb (1 Cor 16:13). He paired it with a verb meaning "be strong." We may well understand fortitude as the virtue that has enabled many faithful Christians to become martyrs for Christ's sake.

The ancient Greeks had an incredible vision for the kind of people and the kind of cities they believed were desirable, possible, and achievable. They believed whole populations could learn to act with understanding (prudence); with fair dealings (justice); with self-control (temperance); and with courage (fortitude). What an optimistic view of human nature! Today's reality falls far short.

The earliest Christians had a more robust understanding of the debilitating effects of sin on individuals and on societies. They knew that natural morality is neither achievable nor adequate. Thus, Jesus and the apostles taught that genuine character development occurs only because the Spirit enables. Many non-Christians exert the cardinal virtues to a degree or for a season, yet we are all naturally disinclined to become people with these qualities. Only as we are strengthened by the power of the Spirit will these virtues become ours in increasing measure.

The Three Theological Virtues

Then there are the virtues that are so supernatural and so closely associated with Christianity that they must be understood entirely as gifts of God's grace. The church fathers took their cue from Paul in identifying three character traits that are found only in a genuine relationship with Christ: "And now these three remain: faith, hope and love. But the greatest of these is love" (1 Cor 13:13).

Faith (Greek pistis). Trust; belief; commitment to God and his Word with obedience to him implied. The noun "faith" or "trust" is found more than 240 times in the New Testament; the related verb ("believe" or "have faith") also occurs more than 240 times. At once we know that we are dealing with an entirely different—and vastly more important—quality than for any of the cardinal virtues. Three texts epitomize the centrality of faith for followers of Jesus.

- Importance of faith for salvation, John 3:16.
- Definition and outworking of faith, Hebrews 11:1, 6.
- Relationship between faith and good works, James 2:22–23.

"Belief" (both noun and verb) are widely used in a variety of biblical contexts. Yet the following points are clear enough.

- Christian faith necessarily includes belief in the existence of God as revealed in Scripture.
- Christian faith necessarily includes belief in Jesus of Nazareth as a historical person and commitment to his teachings in the Gospels.
- Faith was a central teaching of Jesus regarding the good news (the gospel). There is no meaningful understanding of Christianity apart from committing oneself to Jesus.

- Christian faith necessarily includes affirming that Jesus's death by crucifixion has saving value: "Christ died for our sins."
- Christian faith requires belief that Jesus was resurrected bodily from the dead.

The following points regarding faith have been widely discussed, yet there is room for disagreement among Christian thinkers.

- Faith is closely related to knowledge. It is not a blind leap in the dark. Yet the exact relationship between faith and facts is open to interpretation.
- Faith includes "confidence in" as well as "belief that."
- Distinctions have often been between historical faith (assenting to certain facts), temporal faith (believing that God will work in a situation, such as physical healing), and saving faith.

Hope (Greek elpis). Confident expectation of receiving what God has promised. New Testament writers used the noun hope more than fifty times; they used the related verb about thirty times. Hope is not as prominent in Scripture as faith or love; nevertheless, it stands as one of the three crowning virtues. In the Christian sense, hope is based in God and his character (1 Pet 1:21). An important aspect of biblical hope is its orientation to the future. Hope looks forward to the return of Christ to complete God's purposes. The "blessed hope" of Jesus's followers is Christ's second coming (Titus 2:13).

Hope as a virtue is differs greatly from psychological hope, which is usually understood as a feeling that what is desired will happen. Such hope may have temporary value as an antidote for dejection or despair, just as temporal faith may give individuals a sense of purpose. Christian hope, however, is God's great gift regarding our eternal future (Heb 6:19).

Love (Greek agape). Giving oneself to others; freely given, intense affection expressing delight and goodwill for the beloved; the greatest virtue, because God is love. The thing to be said at once is that love is not a feeling or emotion (passion). Rather, love—like all the other virtues—is centered in one's inner self. Forms of "love" are found throughout the New Testament. The noun is found more than 110 times; the adjective (traditionally translated "beloved") occurs more than 60 times; and the verb form occurs more than 140 times. Strikingly, forms of agape were rarely used by the ancient Greeks. Agape is a Christian-specific virtue. The roots of the Christian understanding of love go back to the love of God in the Old Testament (Hebrew chesed, traditionally translated "lovingkindness"). Because of his love, he reached out to Israel and made them his covenant people. The New Testament writers continued the theme, but even more strongly: "God is love" (1 John 4:8). "God is love" is true because he exists eternally as the Godhead of three persons who love each other endlessly.

Jesus emphasized the centrality of love in many ways. Two of his essential teachings focus on the supremacy of love for his followers. First is the commandment to love one another (John 13:34–35). Second is his restatement of the two "great commandments" (Matt 11:37–40, citing Deut 6:5 and Lev 19:18). Other chapters in the present book expand the centrality of love as the greatest of the fruit of the Spirit.

Our journey toward godliness includes giving diligent attention to building a life of virtue. With the ancient Greeks, we join in affirming that a life of character takes a lifetime of endeavor. Yet with the church fathers, we say that a life of character is also the gift of God's grace. The fruit of the Spirit begins to be developed both by sustained effort and by God's mysterious inner work. Because faith, hope, and love are eternal, everlasting life includes continued growing in virtue throughout all eternity.

Reflective Questions

- How important is it for you to identify virtues in which you would like to grow?
- Should we expect those who are not disciples to grow in character? Why or why not?
- Why are faith, hope, and love the greatest of the fruit of the Spirit? Is love really the greatest?

SPIRITUAL HEALTH
(LUNCH WITH THE SPIRIT)

I've reached the life stage in which an annual physical examination is essential. Because I've been healthy as an adult, I was shocked several years ago when the results of a routine exam suggested I might be diabetic. Sure enough, further tests demonstrated my body no longer processes sugar well. Oral medications, as well as attention to diet and exercise, have been effective. But I must pay close attention, and now I have to check my blood sugar daily with my trusty glucose meter. A couple of years later, my routine EKG suggested a possible heart irregularity. A visit to a cardiologist, coupled with a treadmill test, indicated that my heart is just fine. Staying healthy requires work!

From a physical point of view, no adults should assume they'll always be healthy. The same is true with our spiritual lives, especially when we recognize that many forces loose in today's world threaten to undo us. Peter Scazzero's Emotionally Healthy

Spirituality has particularly brought to the forefront the importance of emotional health for growing in Christlikeness. Frankly, some believers—even leaders and those who have followed Christ for decades—remain unaware of issues that may be making them spiritually sick, just as I was unaware of my diabetes (which had begun several years earlier).

External Factors that Threaten Spiritual Health

In his parable of the sower, Jesus described seed that fell among thorns and failed to produce a harvest. The culprits were "the worries of this age and the deceitfulness of wealth" (Matt 13:22). The apostle John identified the threats coming from the world as "the lust of the flesh, the lust of the eyes, and the pride in one's possessions" (1 John 2:16). So it is that "the world" pulls at us and often we become unbalanced by unhealthy patterns that make us sick.

The push to perform. Some of us may become so career oriented, whether in the marketplace or in Christian ministry, that we define ourselves by what we do and how successful we are. We seek approval as proven by increasing numbers (more sales; more members; more giving). Instead of remembering that we are human beings, we function as human doings. When we focus our lives on what we are doing, either for God or our employer, rather than cultivating a relationship with (or better yet, feasting with) the

Father, Son, and Spirit, we have become spiritually sick.

Addictions to substances. The world offers alluring traps that hook us. One of the oldest is the appeal of alcohol. Scripture warned against drunkenness because of its horrifying effects on both the users and those around them. Too many followers of Jesus have followed the understandable appeal of social drinking into the trap of addiction. Then there's the newer siren song of drugs, whether legal or illegal. Well-meaning believers have allowed themselves to become dependent on pain-killing drugs, originally prescribed for legitimate reasons. Unfortunately, Jesus's disciples are not exempt from the lure of tobacco, marijuana, or street drugs. All these are known to affect our bodies negatively. In some instances, the addiction remains largely hidden; in other cases, all becomes known.

Addiction to pornography. As soon as the printing press was perfected, pornographic books found a market. As soon as moving pictures were invented, porn flicks became available in adult theaters. With the arrival of the internet, personal computers, and mobile devices, the most lurid adult materials are instantly available with one or two taps or mouse clicks. Believers appear to view porn at similar rates as others. Further, tawdry "soft-porn" romance novels titillate with portrayals of idealized sexual fulfillment. Porn consumers know that they are heaping up shame and guilt. This often harms those closest to them: spouse and children.

Keeping up with the Joneses. Chasing the American dream can lead to overextending ourselves financially or neglecting sacrificial generosity. As we choose our lifestyle, intentionally or by default, whether suburban or urban or rural, we may be living more like the general culture than we care to admit. Have we become materialists? Is credit card debt killing us? Do we invest more time in secondary pursuits (clubs, hobbies, sports) than in God's kingdom? If so, we have become spiritually unhealthy.

As you have read through these external factors that can threaten spiritual health, you may very well have found that one or more hits the mark. Or some other issue may have percolated into your consciousness. I've given only a suggested list. Before we consider ways to defeat external threats, consider what may be even more damaging: internal factors.

Internal Factors That Threaten Spiritual Health

The ancient Hebrew prophet lamented, "The heart is more deceitful than anything else, and incurable—who can understand it?" (Jer 17:9). Jesus was equally harsh: "From within come evil thoughts, sexual immoralities, thefts, murders, adulteries, greed, evil actions, deceit, self-indulgence, envy, slander, pride, and foolishness. All these evil things come from within and defile a person" (Mark 7:21–22). Yes, through regeneration we become new in Christ. Yes, through justification we have been declared right with God. But the old habits and tendencies away from God are not instantly removed when we become followers of Jesus. It takes a lifetime to deal with some of these. Unresolved, these cause us to live in a state of "dis-ease."

Living in anger or fear. Let's face it. Some of us by temperament are prone to anger. We explode on others and hurt them (and ourselves) in the process. Others are more even-keeled, whether by temperament or by self-control. Of course, anger has its place; there's a time for legitimate anger. Yet consider these indicators that anger has made us sick: name calling; belittling others; impatience; short temper; blaming others; people avoiding us; people fearful of being around us. Living in anger is a broadly human issue not limited to followers of Jesus. But we believers are expected to live by the instruction, "Be angry and do not sin. Don't let the sun go down on your anger, and don't give the devil an opportunity" (Eph 4:26-27).

Fear, like anger, has a valid place, and when we are faced with sudden danger the "fight or flight" instinct may save our lives. Yet many Christians live with chronic anxiety. This takes many forms. It may be fear that God doesn't really love us. It may be worry over our health or the health of a loved one. It may be fear of failure. Jesus addressed fear—worry or anxiety about God's care for his people—this way: "So don't worry, saying, 'What will we eat?' or 'What will we drink?' . . . Your heavenly Father knows that you need them. But seek first the kingdom of God and his righteousness, and all these things will be provided for you" (Matt 6:31–33).

Unresolved issues from our past. Children may experience traumatic events that they haven't processed very well: divorce; death of a parent or sibling; gender-identity questions; physical or mental abuse; rejection. Some of us have suffered from broken relationships that still hurt: an unfaithful partner; rejection after a debilitating accident or illness; stupidity on our part. Pastors have compared such unresolved issues to an iceberg: there's much more below the surface—with the capacity to cause damage—than is visible. The people of Israel had a proverb about the devastating impact of the failures of parents on their children: "The fathers have eaten sour grapes, and the children's teeth are set on edge" (Jer 31:29; Ezek 18:2). Yet the force of the proverb was not inevitable, as Jeremiah and Ezekiel both explained. We are not doomed by our past. Disciples of Jesus sickened by unresolved issues can find hope that, as they grow in Christlike maturity, health and resolution will be found.

Refusing to acknowledge weakness or failure. All too often we have mastered the art of projecting a persona filled only with success or winning. Our social media feeds can look like film clips titled, "Greatest Hits of My Life." Not everyone spending endless hours on digital devices in seemingly neutral activities (social media, gaming, surfing the internet) is doing so to cover weakness. But it may be so, and internet compulsion has become for many another area of sickness. We become adept at putting on masks so that others don't see the real us. We focus on our heads (intellectual attainment) rather than our hearts (our affections). We fool ourselves by staying busy and concentrating on performance. Jesus's story about the Pharisee and the tax collector (Luke 18:9–14) perfectly illustrates the problem. It's the one who prayed, "God, have mercy on me, a sinner!" who ended up in a state of spiritual health.

Dealing with depression. Feeling blue or discouraged at life circumstances is to be expected. When it lasts for weeks or months, affecting our ability to function normally, then depression may have set in. Depressed people are unable to enjoy the people and activities they once loved. Other symptoms—fatigue, excessive sleep, inability to think clearly—are also common. Depression exists among followers of Jesus at similar rates as for non-Christians. Fortunately, this no longer bears the stigma among Christians it once had. There are chemical factors that may be treated with medication. For some, depression may be a lifetime challenge that can be managed. For others, depression is temporary.

Prescriptions for Spiritual Health

No magic bullet cures exist for the kinds of spiritual sickness identified above. Yet across the centuries, ways to move toward health, with God's help, have been identified. In the paragraphs that follow, I link one workable prescription to each of the eight factors noted. Some of the prescriptions certainly apply to more than one illness factor. But a good place to begin is to note the correlation suggested in what follows.

Embracing spiritual rhythms as a prescription for the push to perform. One helpful way to resist the crazy, busy performance trap is to incorporate spiritual rhythms that push us back toward being rather than doing. God required the Israelites to commit one day in seven to resting. (Worshiping one day in seven came much later.) Many people are rediscovering the spiritual benefits of observing a weekly Sabbath (see Lauren Winner's winsome 2003 book, Mudhouse Sabbath). For an even more robust pathway to focus on spiritual rhythms, consider the ancient Christian practice of "the divine office": following a pattern of structured prayers for every morning and evening. I have been helped immensely through following the prayer practices outlined Phyllis Tickle's The Divine Hours (3 volumes, 2006). Be certain that the Spirit wants you to break free from any pressure to define yourself by performance.

Twelve-step programs as a prescription for addiction to substances. Alcoholics Anonymous, founded in 1935, was the first of the twelve-step programs. Through AA, thousands have journeyed successfully from powerlessness with alcohol to recovery. Other twelve-step groups have addressed newer addictions: Narcotics Anonymous; Marijuana Anonymous; Cocaine Anonymous; Gamblers Anonymous; Sexaholics Anonymous. While these programs are not specifically Christian—although they do appeal to a Higher Power—many followers of Jesus have found recovery through these programs because they addressed the bondage of addiction more rigorously than most churches are equipped to do. Be certain that the Spirit wants you to break free from addiction to substances.

Accountability partners as a prescription for addiction to pornography. No serious-minded follower of Jesus can believe that porn is harmless. It's kept secret and covered up. Multiplied thousands have tried in vain to escape the porn habit. Victory comes at a price. The best ways toward success include coming clean in repentance to God and others; establishing strong digital filters on all internet-connected devices (such as Covenant Eyes or X3watch); and securing an accountability partner who will agree to a weekly discussion (more often if needed) and who will receive reports regarding internet usage, including porn sites. Be certain that the Spirit wants you to break free from addiction to pornography.

Repentance and confession as a prescription for keeping up with the Joneses. The first step toward health in this regard is to admit there's a problem with materialism. It's subtle. But it grabs us. The devil tempted Jesus with the promise of all the world's kingdoms for a "small" price (Matt. 4:8–10). Jesus wasn't fooled. His answer was to worship and serve the Lord God only. He recognized that material stuff can become an idol. We can make what should be secondary (clubs, sports, hobbies, etc.) primary.

When that happens, we're idolaters. The only way to break the "dis-ease" of materialism is to confess it as sin and take steps to forsake it. This is hard. It's countercultural. It will help to have fellow travelers. Studying David Platt's Radical (2010) can be a good step for reconfiguring your priorities. Be certain that the Spirit wants you to break free from the idolatry of materialism and keeping up with the Joneses.

Intentional vulnerability as a prescription for living in anger or fear. Typically, people expressing anger or fear are unwilling to be exposed to the possibility of being attacked or wounded, whether physically or emotionally. Thus, we wall ourselves off. For believers, the beginning point is to seek fresh insight into God's character. Anger at God means that we believe God doesn't love us or that he is not the sovereign Lord of all. This then leads to anger with others: difficulties with people are somehow God's fault. Worry or fear means that we think we can't trust God: he will disappoint us or act in ways we don't approve. This in turn can lead us to worry about others (or even ourselves). When we embrace God's unconditional love and care for us as our Father, then we will risk openness—vulnerability—in our relationship with him. This in turn lays a foundation for openness to others, even when we know we may be wounded. Be certain that the Spirit wants you to break free from living in anger or fear.

Reflection and a conversation partner as a prescription for unresolved issues from our past. A time of introspection about one's childhood or other relational issues from the past is the last thing many of us are willing to do. We have often had years of practicing how to "stuff it." We should not stay stuck in the past, but it's helpful to assess the past occasionally. A conversation partner may be helpful: a trusted spiritual leader, a professional Christian counselor, or a friend willing to journey with us through our past. Chapter 11, "Companionship in Community," offers added insights concerning such companions. Be certain that the Spirit wants you to resolve any past issues and move forward into a healthy spiritual future.

Seeking spiritual consistency as a prescription for refusing to acknowledge weakness or failure. Regular self-reflection about whether we're papering over weaknesses with a tissue-thin appearance of strength and success is an important exercise for spiritual health. But more than just admitting to ourselves (and others) that we have been inauthentic is to make a commitment to grow in consistency. Will we commit to become authentic (honest, real) with others about the extent to which we are truly feasting with the Father (biblical formation, including regular Scripture study and meditation), feasting with the Spirit (spiritual formation, including a focus on spiritual fruit), and feasting with the Son (relational formation, including worshiping with a community of disciples)? If so, be certain that the Spirit wants you to become a spiritually consistent person, honest about personal weakness and failure.

Living with joy as a prescription for dealing with depression. Medications and Christian counseling enable many believers with chronic depression to function normally. For those with either temporary or long-term depression, the challenge is to keep from getting depressed over the depression. Rather, the challenge is to recognize that the Spirit longs to equip every believer with joy for the journey. Focusing on the Lord rather than on the limitations one is facing due to discouragement or depression can provide liberation. If anyone had a reason to be depressed, it was Paul in his long Roman imprisonment, about to face the emperor in a life-or-death case. Read his "cure for depression" in Philippians 1:12–30. Be certain that the Spirit wants you to live with daily joy as you deal with issues of depression you may face.

Reflective Questions: Spiritual Health

- How regularly do you complete a spiritual health checkup? How healthy are you spiritually?
- What allure from the world is most bothersome to you? What allure from your own "flesh"?
- Which "prescriptions" for spiritual health are the most effective in your life? Why?

SPIRITUAL DISCIPLINE
(LUNCH WITH THE SPIRIT)

Athletic success comes at a cost: workouts, hours in the gym, practice, and then more practice. Such hard work is generally just a means to an end. When Paul compared bodily disciplines to spiritual disciplines (1 Tim 4:8), he meant that both require intentionality. We don't naturally choose the gym routine, the 10K run, or the swim practice. But if we do them faithfully, we become better gymnasts or runners or swimmers. We don't on our own choose exercises meant to develop intimacy with Father, Son, and Spirit; but when we pursue such habits of the heart or "sacred rhythms," we progress in godliness. Spiritual discipline is a "menu item" we may prefer to decline. This chapter is meant to persuade you otherwise.

The ancient monastic practices of the classic spiritual disciplines have recently been recovered for non-Catholics by such writers as Richard Foster (Celebration of Discipline: The Path to Spiritual Growth, 1978) and Dallas Willard (The Spirit of the Disciplines: Understanding How God Changes Lives, 1988). They stress that these disciplines cannot be followed legalistically. Unless the Spirit motivates us, we will fail miserably and our spiritual lives will become an intolerable burden. The disciplines are instruments that may help us follow Jesus's instruction, "If anyone wants to follow after me, let him deny himself, take up his cross daily, and follow me" (Luke 9:23). The disciplines open the doors of our heart for the Spirit to transform us; the disciplines themselves are not the same as godliness or spiritual maturity.

There is no standard list of the spiritual disciplines, just as there is no official list of gifts of the Spirit. The following are among the frequently mentioned spiritual habits that godly people throughout the centuries have practiced.

Disciplines of Saying No to Natural Desires

Solitude and silence. Noise pervades our daily lives. Smartphones incessantly tug at us to check for messages. Many apps work like hardcore drugs: we can't wait for the next hit. To make progress in enjoying God's presence, we must limit such pulls. Even our Lord found it important to get away from others where he would not be distracted: "He got up, went out, and made his way to a deserted place; and there he was praying" (Mark 1:35).

There's no set rules for developing patterns of solitude and silence, other than to turn off (or physically remove) electronic sources of information or music: television, radio, smartphone, computer, etc. Some believers get up early, before the rest of the household, for a few moments of stillness before beginning any time of Bible reading or prayer. They often choose a spot in the home as a sacred space. Many (including myself) light a special candle as a visual reminder. Others get out in nature, perhaps on a favorite hiking trail every Saturday morning.

When we're so accustomed to the pull of others, it can be painful, like detox, to move into deliberate times of solitude and silence. Most people begin gradually: two to five minutes of stillness. Setting one's mind on God without a Bible in hand or a prayer list can be difficult at first. But it becomes rewarding. Many find benefit in an all-day silent retreat or even longer. A cabin, a room at a retreat center, or a cemetery are places where you may wait silently for God.

Fasting and chastity. We were born with two God-given appetites: the desire for food and the desire for sex. Yet these desires can be misused. Anorexia, bulimia, and obesity are food disorders that many struggle with. What used to be considered abuse or perversion of the sex drive is now often celebrated in society, but the biblical teaching about both drives is clear.

The people of Israel were ordered to fast—abstain from food but not water—only one day a year, the Day of Atonement (Lev 23:27). Other fasts were voluntary. Jesus fasted forty days as a spiritual discipline, and in the Sermon on the Mount he said "whenever you fast" not "if you fast" (Matt 6:16). Voluntary fasting as a spiritual exercise is a way of denying bodily demands so that we may give additional attention to God.

It ought to go without saying that followers of Jesus are committed to expressing sexual intimacy only within the bond of heterosexual marriage. For many, this commitment may itself be a spiritual discipline to be learned. Other followers of Jesus have been called to a lifetime of sexual abstinence (Matt 19:12), as strange as that sounds today. Further, within marriage sexual abstinence is suitable, by agreement and for only a limited time (1 Cor 7:5).

The best way to ease into fasting is to bypass two meals, for example, eating a normal supper, and then not eating again until supper the following day. Time normally spent eating may be spent in prayer or other spiritual engagement. For special purposes—to seek God's face for a serious need—longer fasts are appropriate. Jesus asked us to keep fasting private, between ourselves and God. The exception is when a group—a congregation or a family—agrees to fast for a specific purpose. Those who are part of church in which the season of Lent or Advent is recognized may wish to participate in a partial fast during these times, for example, giving up caffeine or dessert or meat. Again, the purpose is spiritual, not dietary.

Simplicity and frugality. Many friends have expressed to me they wished they knew how to simplify and not feel that they must keep more and more plates spinning. That's where intentional simplicity comes into its own. The previous chapter mentioned materialism as an indication of spiritual "dis-ease." Jesus spoke about seeking the kingdom first, not being anxious, and trusting God to provide what is necessary (Matt. 6:25–34). The heart of simplicity is to live with an awareness that everything we have received is a gift from God. When we think of ourselves as stewards of God's gifts, rather than owners of our "stuff," we become free to give our things to others. Simplicity is also an attitude applicable to our speech. Jesus counseled, "Let your 'yes' mean 'yes,' and your 'no' mean 'no.' Anything more than this is from the evil one" (Matt 5:37; see also Eccl 5:2).

The inner commitment to simplicity will best be expressed by an outward commitment to frugality: being prudent or economical in using resources, avoiding waste or extravagance. Frugality will be demonstrated variously, depending on our overall economic situation. But let's face it, do we really need that daily five-dollar latte? What do we gain by trading in our vehicle or our phone every two years for the next model with newer bells and whistles? There are certainly appropriate times for extravagance. The father of the prodigal celebrated by killing the fattened calf. Jesus made lots of wine at the wedding at Cana. Paul expressed the heart of frugality when he wrote: "I know both how to make do with little, and I know how to make do with a lot. In any and all circumstances, I have learned the secret of being content. . . . I am able to do all things through him who strengthens me" (Phil 4:12–13).

Disciplines of Opening the Heart to God Personally

Study and journaling. Scripture was the focus of chapter 4. The material there dealing with "disciplined study of the Bible" need not be repeated here. Thanks to the printing press and the translation of Scripture into our language—a wonderful product of the Reformation—we may study to show ourselves approved to God as those who handle the Word well (2 Tim 2:15). Personal investigation of Scripture is undoubtedly the chief way that God speaks to us. Yet there are additional ways of studying Scripture: small groups, academic institutions, and even Sunday school.

The results of study will be lost unless there is a way of preserving one's gains. That's where journaling comes in. It's a discipline that requires great intentionality. It's very difficult for me personally. Some use small books (such as Moleskine). Some use a computer or other digital device. Further, journaling is not limited to the result of Bible study. Many keep journals as a prayer log or to record the ways they are interacting with God or others. Success in journaling is a matter of taking the first step and then asking God for the grace to keep at it.

Meditation and contemplation. For many Christians, "meditation" sounds like Eastern mysticism: assuming a lotus position and reciting mantras to empty the mind. Christian meditation and contemplation are about filling the mind and heart with

God's presence. Further, they are not merely psychological techniques to lower stress or blood pressure.

By meditation I am here referring to the practice of sacred reading of Scripture sketched in chapter 4: soaking in a brief passage, listening quietly for what the Spirit wants to convey personally and subjectively. Other spiritual works are worthy of slow, careful reading and listening for to God speak through them. Augustine's Confessions, Bunyan's Pilgrim's Progress, and C. S. Lewis's Mere Christianity are examples.

The heart of contemplation is to seek to gaze upon or to behold God himself with one's spiritual eyes. Jesus promised, "Blessed are the pure in heart, for they will see God" (Matt 5:8). A person doesn't see God just by wanting to. Paul prayed for the Ephesians that "the eyes of your heart may be enlightened" (Eph 1:18). Contemplation comes as the crescendo after we have gained experience in solitude, silence, and meditation. It is a matter of focusing—often using the imagination—on a single truth about God and reflecting intensely. A few examples will help.

- **God's yearning for rebels.** Imagine the story of the prodigal son; picture yourself in the story; use Henri Nouwen's *The Return of the Prodigal Son* as a guide for meditation.
- **God's creative beauty.** Pluck a leaf from a tree and look closely at its intricate struc-

tures; snorkel off a tropical beach; observe children romping on a playground.
- **God's sacrifice of his Son.** Sit alone in a chapel, focusing on a cross or other depiction of Jesus's death; listen to music such as Bach's *Mass in B Minor* or part 2 of Handel's *Messiah*.

Prayer and secrecy. Prayer is our speaking to God, just as Scripture study and meditation are ways in which God speaks. Scripture is filled with encouragement to pray. Prayer may precede or follow—or be in the middle of—Scripture study and meditation. As with the previous disciplines, the focus is on personal action: "When you pray, go into your private room, shut your door, and pray to your Father who is in secret" (Matt 6:6). Corporate prayer, in families or in public worship or other gatherings, is certainly called for; yet it's private prayer that Scripture encourages as primary. The effectiveness of corporate prayer depends on how diligently those gathered have first engaged God in the "prayer closet." For those beginning the journey of prayer, a helpful guide may be found in the acronym A.C.T.S.

- **Adoration.** Prayer appropriately begins with praising God for who he is, his greatness and his goodness. The book of Psalms is the Bible's prayer book that teaches this approach.

- **Confession.** We approach God with awareness of our own sins, asking humbly for his mercy and forgiveness (1 John 1:9).
- **Thanksgiving.** When we "count our blessings," we overflow with thankfulness to God, not only for his providential care over his creation but for his gifts that accompany salvation.
- **Supplication.** Now we are ready to beseech God on behalf of ourselves and others, letting our requests be made known to God, who longs to answer the petitions of his children.

Secrecy means keeping our personal spiritual exercises private. Jesus asked for secrecy not only in prayer but also in the disciplines of fasting and stewardship. We are forbidden to seek the praise of people in our devotion to God, so much so that we do not let our left hand know what our right hand is doing, as if that were possible (Matt. 6:4). What balances this secrecy is our public actions, done as "salt and light" in our witness and service to others.

Disciplines of Engaging Others

Worship and fellowship. Part 3 of this book focuses on relational formation: the centrality of sharing life with others in our journey toward Christlikeness. Thus, the comments here serve as a transition to part 3. The story of the God's people, both in the Bible as well as in Christian history, supposes that we are in relationship with God not as solitary individuals but as "the people of God." A robust understanding of the church includes the importance of assemblies for worship. (The Greek word ekklēsia, traditionally translated "church," may better be rendered "assembly.") The central purpose for congregational life is worship or glorifying God (see chapter 1).

The main New Testament term for fellowship is based on the Greek term koinōnia, essentially referring to sharing together or having things in common. In the Gospels, Jesus laid the foundation by designating the Twelve and some women disciples to travel with him (Luke 8:1–3). The book of Acts testifies that fellowship was a joyful highlight of early congregations.

Confession and accountability. Repentance (turning away from sins) and confession (acknowledging to God and others that we have sinned and long to be forgiven) were noted in the previous chapter. So was the concept of accountability. As we saw, these disciplines are ways the Spirit may work to help bring health to specific areas of spiritual "dis-ease." Here, the big idea is that confession to an individual or to a group is a spiritual discipline that will help us grow: "Confess your sins to one another and pray for one another" (Jas 5:16). A wide spectrum of confession practices has developed over the centuries. In some traditions, confession is primarily or exclusively between the individual and God. In other traditions, confession to another Christian—usually a church leader—has become a mandatory practice, particularly before the Lord's Supper. In yet other traditions, corporate confession and absolution are part of the Sunday liturgy. In any case, a wise practice is that the "circle of confession" should generally be the same as the "circle of sin"; that is, we are to confess our specific sins principally to those directly affected by our sins. Yet throughout the centuries, believers have attested the spiritual value of confessing sins regularly to a trusted Christian friend.

Closely related to having a "confessor" is having an "accountability partner," someone of the same gender who has the right to ask us hard questions about behaviors and sin patterns and who agrees to a regular time of mutual sharing. Usually, the questions that may be asked will be known ahead of time. The process of accountability will change and develop over time. As such spiritual friends grow in trust and respect for each other, they may well reach a level of commitment in which each is free to call on the other in any situation at any time.

Service and stewardship. Jesus declared that the second most important command in Scripture is, "Love your neighbor as yourself" (Mark 12:31; Lev 19:18). He also taught, "Love your enemies" (Matt 5:44). Growing in Christlikeness therefore necessarily includes serving our neighbors—fellow believers—motivated by love, as well as serving those who are not our neighbors, even those who hate us. Both Testaments are filled with examples as well as exhortations along these lines. Serving is best done not as a solitary individual but in community. As followers of Jesus work together, we are more effective at meeting needs, both of those inside and those apart from our congregation.

An important, even essential, corollary of giving our time and energy is serving through generous giving. This is directly related to the discipline of frugality, noted earlier in this chapter. Simply put, those who choose to live frugally have more financial resources to give to the needs of their own congregation and others. The most extensive teaching about stewardship is Paul's advice to the Christians of Corinth, whom he urged to give sacrificially to help poverty-stricken believers in Jerusalem (2 Cor 8–9). His most famous advice to them: "Each person should do as he has decided in his heart—not reluctantly or out of compulsion, since God loves a cheerful giver" (2 Cor 9:7).

Reflective Questions

- How willing are you to embrace spiritual practices from the world of monasteries?
- In what ways are you practicing self-denial as part of taking up your cross daily?
- What steps could you take to foster the biblical practices of meditation (deep reflection on Scripture) and contemplation (seeking to behold God's presence)?

PART 3

SUPPER WITH THE SON, OR RELATIONAL FORMATION

Christian maturity is impossible isolated from other followers of Jesus. The church is his body; he is head of the body. The supper focus, relational formation, is the Son whom we worship together with others. He has called us grow in relationship with others so that we may better live out both the great commission and the great commandments. Here's what's served on the menu.

Worship in community. There is only one church in the world, but the New Testament emphasizes local assemblies. Christian worship has historically been organized around the Lord's Supper and proclaiming the Word. Whether we are formal or informal, ancient, modern, or contemporary in liturgy, shared worship is essential for spiritual growth.

Companionship in community. Fellowship has long been admired as an essential part of congregational life, yet often Sunday gatherings are merely individuals occupying the same room. Genuine companionship is possible and desirable, but we must be intentional. The companions we enjoy typically follow the three "natural" loves (affection, eros, and friendship). Ultimately, however, Christian community depends on *agapē*.

Mission in community. The primary mission of the local church is clear from the New Testament: to bear witness to Jesus and to make disciples of all nations. Although parachurch organizations assist congregations in the tasks of evangelism and mission, congregations are to give thoughtful attention to the equip members to witness effectively for Christ.

Service in community. Only in relationship with other Christians can we truly fulfill the great commandments: love God and love our neighbors. Jesus provides the example of loving service to others, and Christians have historically been involved in serving society at large. Together, leaders and members of congregations decide how to address ministry needs.

WORSHIP IN COMMUNITY (SUPPER WITH THE SON)

Christ invites us to feast with him by joining others in worshiping him as our Lord and Savior. We "sup with the Son" when we worship him in the presence of others. To a woman who was ethnically an outsider and of questionable moral character, Jesus said, "An hour is coming, and is now here, when the true worshipers will worship the Father in Spirit and in truth. Yes, the Father wants such people to worship him" (John 4:23). Our Lord was affirming that God means for people to worship him, but only when we worship him right. Further, this text implies that worship is primarily a shared opportunity. Individualistic worship is possible, but worship happens best in community.

Further, just because God's people are engaged in acts of worship doesn't mean that genuine worship is occurring. The Lord through Isaiah criticized the Israelites who "approach me with their speeches to honor me with lip service—yet their hearts are far from me, and human rules direct their worship of me" (Isa 29:13). Even sadder, people may be worshiping idolatrously even though they think their object of worship is the true God. When the Israelites worshiped a gold calf statue, they claimed it was a festival to the Lord (Exod 32).

Worship in the New Testament emphasizes believers of the same local congregation who gather in devotion to Jesus Christ. Thus, although there is only "one holy catholic and apostolic church"—the worldwide, throughout-time company of the redeemed—worship is a local church responsibility. Christian worship does not center on a building (the temple) or ancient Israelite rituals involving animal sacrifice (such as Passover). So what does it mean to worship "in Spirit and in truth," that is, worship motivated by the Spirit and carried out according to gospel truth?

Christian Worship in the New Testament

The earliest statement about Christian worship notes four elements: "They devoted themselves to the apostles' teaching, to the fellowship, to the breaking of bread, and to prayer" (Acts 2:42). This is not necessarily a normative text, but it does provide helpful pointers. "The apostles' teaching" has come to us in the form of written texts: the New Testament. Scripture is always important if not essential when followers of Jesus gather in his name. "The fellowship" refers to life together, developed in detail in the next chapter. "The breaking of bread" means either shared meals or the Lord's Supper. Whether a shared meal is in mind (as in Mark 6:41; 8:6) or the Lord's Supper (1 Cor. 10:16; 11:24) is not important for the present discussion. "Prayer" refers to corporate adoration of our Lord and petition to him. Acts 20:7–12 describes a worship gathering by believers in Troas on the first day of the week, in honor of Jesus's resurrection on the first day of the week, to hear an apostle teach and to break bread together.

The epistles sketch out apostolic instructions for worship. The following may be noted:

1. Sharing the Lord's Supper (1 Cor 11:17–26), to be carried out "as often as you eat this bread and drink the cup."
2. Exercising spiritual gifts (1 Cor 12:1–14:40), to be carried out "decently and in order."
3. Contributing financially (1 Cor 16:2; 2 Cor 8–9) to meet the needs of others.
4. Making a rich place for the Word (Col 3:16) by teaching and encouraging each other.
5. Singing together (Eph 5:19; Col 3:16) with psalms, hymns, and spiritual songs.
6. Praying together (1 Tim 2:1–4, 8) both with thanksgiving and with intercession.

It's not often remembered that Revelation is a book of worship, filled with hymns to and about

Christ. While Revelation's worship scenes are often heavenly, they are surely meant as indications of ways followers of Jesus are to worship him on earth.

1. John worshiped "in the Spirit on the Lord's day" (Rev. 1:10) when he was overwhelmed by a vision of the exalted Jesus.
2. Worship on earth—especially the prayers of God's people—make a direct impact in the very throne room of God, like great bowls of incense (Rev 5:8).
3. True worship includes praise of the Father and the Son equally (Rev. 4–5), both for the work of creation and for the work of redemption.
4. Worship celebrations offer "hallelujahs" for God's great rule and judgment (Rev 19:1–7).

Two Central Features of Worship

The New Testament is clear, and Christian history confirms, that two elements have always been considered indispensable for genuine worship by followers of Jesus gathered on the Lord's Day, Sunday. Although true worship may occur without one (or both) of these, there is great consensus about the centrality of the proclamation of Christ through sermon (the "apostles' teaching") and Supper (the "breaking of bread") as normative.

The ordinances. Jesus commanded—ordained—two rituals for his people. The first was water baptism, an initiation ceremony expected of all who follow him (Matt 28:19). It parallels circumcision of Israelite boy babies on their eighth day as an initiation ceremony expected of all Jews. Sadly, throughout the centuries debates have raged about baptism. (1) Who is a proper candidate, one who personally confesses Jesus as Lord and Savior or a child whose parents confess that they will rear that child within the Christian community? (2) What is the proper mode, immersion or sprinkling or pouring? (3) Who may administer baptism, any previously baptized disciple or only a leader officially consecrated? (4) What is the meaning of the ceremony, a symbol carried out in obedience to Christ or a sacrament that conveys God's grace available in no other way? These debates cannot be settled here, so I must be content to affirm my own commitment to the first answer listed in the questions above. In the history of the church, water baptism, however practiced and understood, has been a prerequisite for participation in the Lord's Supper. In other words, only those who have been properly initiated should participate in the fellowship ceremony.

Second, Jesus commanded—ordained—his followers to reenact parts of his last meal before he died, when he shared with the Twelve bread and cup: "Do this in remembrance of me" (Luke 22:19; 1 Cor 11:24, 25). The primary New Testament term is "the Lord's Supper" (1 Cor 11:20). Some use the term

"Communion" based on Paul's teaching that the Lord's Supper is a "sharing in" or "fellowship with" (Greek, koinōnia) the body of Christ (1 Cor 10:16). Others call it "the Eucharist" based on the Greek verb for giving thanks (eucharisteō), referring to Jesus's thanksgiving for the bread and the cup when he instituted this ordinance (1 Cor 11:23–24). Other terms such as "the Sacrament of the Table" or "Mass" have been adopted by certain denominations, but these phrases come from tradition rather than Scripture.

This ordinance has been the subject of as many debates as baptism throughout the centuries. The most noteworthy questions are as follows. (1) What is the meaning of the ritual, is it a symbolic representation of Jesus's death and believers' participation in his death, or is Jesus Christ spiritually present in a unique way in the Supper, or is this a sacrament that conveys God's grace and Christ's very body and blood available in no other way? (2) How often should baptized Christians, gathered for worship, participate in the Lord's Supper, weekly, monthly, quarterly, annually, or some other frequency? These debates cannot be settled here, so I must be content to affirm my own commitment to the first answer listed in the questions above.

The proclamation of the Word. The Jewish people developed a pattern for worship in their synagogues each Sabbath, which provided a partial template for Christian worship each Lord's Day. This pattern included reading from Scripture and teaching from that text (see Luke 4:16–30). Paul took advantage of this practice to proclaim Jesus through Scripture during his travels (Acts 13:13–41). Christians followed suit. Their Bible was the Old Testament. As the twenty-seven books of the New Testament were written, circulated, and at last universally recognized (by AD 400), they were equally read and taught in Christian worship.

We have already seen that several gifts of the Spirit relate to proclaiming God's truth (prophecy and teaching, for example). As almost his last written words, Paul encouraged Timothy, his younger colleague in ministry: "Preach the word; be ready in season and out of season; rebuke, correct, and encourage with great patience and teaching" (2 Tim 4:2). One of the glories of the Reformation was a recovery of preaching the Word of God, aided by the newfound commitment to translate Scripture into the language of ordinary people.

Sermon and Supper stand as central for worshiping Christians, whether in homes or storefronts or cathedrals or big-box megachurches. Historically, as soon as believers began erecting edifices for people to gather for public worship, the pulpit and the table became the primary articles of furniture, symbolizing that this was indeed a place for *Christian* worship.

Other Important Elements of Worship in Community

As we think beyond sermon and Supper as regular aspects of Christian worship, other features have figured prominently, both in Scripture and in Christian tradition.

Prayer. The previous chapter regarding spiritual discipline focused on personal prayer. But Christian gatherings usually include times of prayer. Sometimes the prayers are spontaneous, "as the Spirit leads" (Acts 4:24-30). Sometimes such prayers are planned ahead of time, and in some traditions prayers are read aloud, such as calls to worship or benedictions. The Lord's Prayer has been memorized and recited collectively as part of public worship down through the centuries. Other memorized prayers have been developed, depending on denominational heritage.

Singing. The book of Psalms (the "Psalter") was the hymnbook of the first Christians, following Jewish custom (Mark 14:26). The New Testament contains several hymns to or about Christ (Phil 2:6–11; Col 1:15–20; Rev 5:12–13). Congregational singing, choirs, "praise teams," and soloists may all be included in Christian worship. Little is stated about the musical instruments that accompany singing, and great variety has developed in the history of churches. Printed hymnals have taken their place alongside Bibles as the two books available in every pew or seat in many Christian worship places.

Giving. Tithes (ten percent as a minimum) were specified for the Israelites in the Old Testament. Generous, sacrificial giving is part of New Testament worship. The Corinthian believers were asked to make their contribution when they gathered on the first day of the week (1 Cor 16:2).

Fellowship. The next chapter develops this theme in more detail, focusing on community or life together outside the time of gathering for worship. Regularly, however, corporate worship includes interacting with others. Worship is not limited to paying attention to those who are "up front." Some churches provide open spaces for mingling before or after worship gatherings; others provide opportunities for greeting one another: shaking hands, sharing hugs, or "passing the peace" as a designated part of the service.

What about Liturgical Worship?

Many of us shrink back, shuddering when we think about worship elements such as lighted candles or processions by robed choirs or ministers. Others shrink back, shuddering when we think about worship including spontaneous elements such as long times of extemporaneous prayer or an unexpected testimonial. To be truthful, both are examples of "liturgy." Liturgy (Greek, leitourgia, "work of the people," 2 Cor 9:12; Phil 2:17) in the broadest sense refers to the customary public worship of a religious group. So, whatever happens on Sunday when followers of Jesus come together is liturgy.

Nevertheless, by customary usage, a congregation that follows a standardized order of service—often indicated by a printed bulletin—is "liturgical." A Christian gathering that is unscripted or spontaneous is "non-liturgical." Certainly, different denominations have established their own patterns concerning the extent to which gathered worship is liturgical. Non-denominational congregations obviously have greater freedom to develop their own liturgical practices than those who participate in a tradition with a fixed liturgy.

One advantage of following a denominational liturgy is that those who established standardized elements for public worship gave thoughtful attention to all the elements that should be included. Consider, for example, The Book of Common Prayer. On the other hand, non-liturgical worship services often demonstrate the lively presence of God's Spirit in ways not evident in more standardized services.

The liturgical year. One valuable aspect of liturgical worship is following the liturgical calendar, a way of marking important days for Christians on an annual basis. Thus, almost all Christians, liturgical or not, recognize Christmas and Easter (the birth and resurrection of Jesus) as special times for worship and celebration. Very early in Christian history these two celebrations began to be preceded by a season of spiritual preparation. Thus, the Christian New Year begins with Advent (a season beginning four Sundays before December 25), culminating with Christmas Day. Also prominent is Lent (a season beginning on Ash Wednesday, forty days before Palm Sunday), culminating in Holy Week, including Good Friday, leading to Easter. Forty days after Easter, many Christians remember Jesus's ascension. Then ten days later comes Pentecost, celebrating the gift of the Holy Spirit.

Both Advent and Lent are times in which all followers of Jesus can practice spiritual disciplines such as fasting and confession. In these ways we may break the chokehold of "the holidays" and "spring break" that dominate the cultural frenzies that Christmas and Easter have evolved into. Advent and Lent are rightly seasons for an entire congregation, but Christians whose churches do not participate in the liturgical year may still participate individually.

Depending on one's denominational tradition, additional festivals are often celebrated. Just as the Israelites benefited from their annual cycle of worship festivals (Passover, Weeks, Booths, etc.), so Christians certainly benefit from knowing we participate in the cycle of worship celebrations established in the early Christian centuries.

Earthly Worship as a Prelude to Eternity

Glorifying God and enjoying him forever is "the chief end of man," as we learned in chapter 1. Worship in community is practice for what we will be doing forever and ever as the redeemed and resurrected people of God. The last two chapters of Revelation envision eternity in terms of a new heaven and a new earth, with "the new Jerusalem" as the centerpiece. It is the place where "God's dwelling is with humanity, and he will live with them. They will be his peoples, and God himself will be with them and be their God" (Rev 21:3). Further, "the throne of God and of the Lamb will be in the city, and his servants will worship him. They will see his face, and his name will be on their foreheads" (Rev 22:3–4).

As we have seen, Christian worship has historically been organized around two central focuses: The Lord's Supper and proclamation of the Word. Whether we are formal or informal, ancient, modern, or contemporary in our liturgy, corporate worship shapes us toward Christlikeness in ways that do not occur in our lives as individuals.

Reflective Questions: Worship in Community

- For you, is worshiping with others about what you get out of it or about praising Christ?
- Why are two central elements of worship proclamation through sermon and the Supper?
- How do you respond to those who claim to love Jesus but don't like the church?

COMPANIONSHIP IN COMMUNITY
(SUPPER WITH THE SON)

Christ invites us to join in feasting with him through companions he provides. We "sup with the Son" in fellowship, not isolation. When I was growing up, the facilities of the congregations we were part of typically had three main sections: the sanctuary (or auditorium) for Sunday worship, the education wing for Sunday school and nursery and choir practice and the church offices, and the fellowship hall (with a kitchen at one end, and often with a basketball court overlaid). We used the fellowship hall for Wednesday night suppers and church-wide potluck dinners and church-league basketball. In my mind, fellowship was what happened in that room or what happened in the fifteen minutes between Sunday school and the worship service (with donuts and juice or coffee). Only much later did I come to understand that true fellowship is broader and deeper than my early experience suggested.

The discussion in chapter 8 about spiritual disciplines included "worship and fellowship" under the heading "disciplines of engaging others." Having considered worship in chapter 9, we now look at fellowship, or as I am calling it here, companionship. Too often, Sunday gatherings involve individuals merely occupying the same room. Those present are no more connected than if they were the random group at the 7:00 p.m. screening of the latest sci-fi thriller at the multiplex cinema. This is perhaps especially the case for more liturgical worship gatherings and for Sunday services in a megachurch setting, even if opportunity is given for greeting—perfunctorily—those seated nearby.

It's been widely observed that many adults have made the claim, "I love Jesus, but I can't stand the church." This comment reflects, sadly, that genuine companionship as part of congregational life has often been short-circuited. Those who desire fellowship don't receive it just because they say they want it. Fellowship is a discipline about which intentionality is the key. Fortunately, genuine companionship is possible—and it is desirable as a vital element in growing toward Christlike maturity. This truth is developed in what may be the most influential book about Christian community ever penned, Dietrich Bonhoeffer's Life Together. (The original work in German was published in 1939, when Bonhoeffer was teaching for a hidden seminary during the time of the Nazis. The English translation was published in 1954.) Further, Bonhoeffer's book shows that often

Christian "life together" is experienced by believers who find community in parachurch contexts, such as Christian colleges or ecumenical Bible study or fellowship groups. The ideal remains, however, that community is best experienced by those who are committed to the same local congregation.

Barnabas, Silas, and Timothy

One of my pastor friends remarked one day in passing, "I think every Christian, like Paul, at times needs a Barnabas, at times needs a Silas, and at times needs a Timothy. Sometimes all three are needed at the same time." He expressed a brilliant insight based on observing the life and ministry of Paul the apostle.

When Paul was a new believer, it was critical for him to have Barnabas as a friend who believed in him, helped him to grow spiritually, and gave him opportunities for ministry (Acts 9:27; 11:29–30). Then these two were sent out together by the church of Antioch. At first Barnabas took the lead, but later he saw the wisdom of letting Paul be in charge of their travels. (Note the subtle shift from "Barnabas and Saul" to "Paul and Barnabas," Acts 13:7, 46.) After these two men parted company, Paul's new partner in ministry became Silas, who served side by side with Paul. They were essentially equals, as the account of establishing the church in Philippi demonstrates (Acts 16). Then came Timothy, whom Paul mentored and gave ministry opportunities, writing him letters and considering him as a son.

As I look back on my life as a follower of Jesus, I had no Barnabas figure in my young-adult years. Hardly ever did anyone older and more mature in the faith take a personal interest in me (with one exception, a beloved college professor). I am certain that I would have made earlier strides to maturity if a seasoned believer had taken me under his wings. On the other hand, I have now benefited greatly from several "Silases." These are men similar in life stage to me. We have agreed to talk and pray and journey together through life, learning to trust each other and to bear each other's burdens. I caught a vision of the importance of "Timothy" relationships when I became a professor at a Christian college and suddenly I was surrounded with young adults, several of whom seemed eager to enter a discipleship relationship with me. These were sometimes one-on-one relationships; sometimes they were small-group relationships. Often, I lost track of these men; for a few of them, I remain in close contact.

As I consider my present season in life, there are three "Silases" that I meet with, one-on-one, on a semi-regular basis. They encourage me because we talk about life-stage issues freely (aging parents; young- adult children). Then there are six "Timothys" that I count as close spiritual friends. Several are young pastors with whom I have a kind of coaching relationship; several others meet with me weekly for Bible study and sharing together. (We are currently working through the life and ministry of Jesus.)

Such relationships do not happen by accident. For the most part, after I have prayed about someone, I have initiated a request: "What would it look like for us to hang out spiritually for a while and see whether the Lord wants to bless our time? Could we meet for coffee, say, every other week for a couple of months to explore journeying with Christ together?" Rarely has someone turned me down flat. Occasionally the connection isn't natural and that's okay. Typically, there has been a gracious, common consent about when the connection—in terms of meeting together regularly—is ready to conclude. I highly recommend that you take the initiative, whether you are looking for a Barnabas, a Silas, or a Timothy. (I'm sorry that I can't find a biblical instance that gives the names of spiritual women who fit this pattern, but I believe this pattern is equally important and valuable for women.) In general, these connections are best kept to the same gender.

Small Groups, Accountability Partners, and Spiritual Directors

In the twentieth century, Sunday school for adults flourished, typically as a small group meeting together for Bible study and fellowship for an hour or so before the worship service. By the last half of the twentieth century, companionship groups were beginning to meet at times other than Sunday mornings and in places other than the church's facilities. These have been called small groups, action groups, fellowship groups, community groups, and, more recently, missional communities. Depending on the church or the parachurch ministry initiating these groups, they have been variously focused. Some stress Bible study; some focus on service projects; other emphases are possible. Adult Sunday school is still a great option in many congregations. The common thread, however, is that these provide the potential for companionship beneficial to spiritual growth.

Chapter 7, on spiritual health, noted that for some followers of Jesus, finding a companion who serves as an accountability partner can be life giving. I have personally benefitted by having such a partner—whom I intentionally sought out—with whom I met weekly. We knew ahead of time the kinds of questions we would ask each other. After we came to trust each other and knew that we were telling the truth in our conversations, we experienced increasing spiritual victory and freedom from some troubling areas of brokenness. For me, having an accountability partner has been encouraging and helpful, but it has also been seasonal, not necessarily an ongoing part of my journey.

In recent decades some Christians have recovered the ancient monastic practice of sustaining a relationship with a spiritual director, someone who probes and offers spiritual exercises as a means of growth. This is not psychotherapy or counseling, which deal mainly with personal relationship issues (the horizontal dimension). Spiritual directors focus on developing a stronger understanding of and love for God (the vertical dimension). It can be challenging to find a spiritual director. Yet those who have spent years with the same spiritual director have testified that the spiritual benefit was tremendous. If you want to learn more about spiritual direction, consider David Benner's Sacred Companions: The Gift of Spiritual Friendship and Direction (2002). In my own case, the ministry and books of Larry Crabb (NewWay Ministries) have been helpful and refreshing along these lines.

Affection, Eros, and Friendship

"The fruit of the Spirit is love" (Gal 5:22). In chapter 6, focusing on spiritual fruit, we saw that "the greatest of these is love" (1 Cor 13:13). The Greek term agapē was traditionally translated "charity," and it is widely acknowledged that our natural loves will fail or fizzle out unless we also encompass agapē: freely given, intense affection expressing delight and goodwill for the beloved.

One of the best discussions of the relationship between agapē and the natural loves is C. S. Lewis's The Four Loves (1960). He made the case that there are three distinct (but sometimes overlapping) loves: affection (Greek, storgē), friendship (Greek, philia), and eros (Greek, eros). All three, when intertwined with agapē, draw us toward godliness; therefore, they are forms of companionship in community. Further, these three loves are to be cherished when they are experienced as part of a local congregation. Reciprocally, church leaders are responsible to encourage growth of these three loves.

Affection. The humblest and most widespread of the natural loves, which comes easy but may be abused, is affection. The easiest example is the universal love of parents for their children and of children for their parents. This kind of affection exists as well between brothers and sisters or among neighbors that we've lived near for many years. We feel a comfortable familiarity with such persons. Like a shabby but favorite reading chair, so we think of those for whom we have affection.

Affection develops among those we are thrown together with, not by deliberate choice but by life circumstances. We didn't choose our parents; they just were our parents. Think about residents on the same floor of a college dormitory; those who work together on an assembly line; those with offices in the same hallway; those on the same high school sports team. Persons like this, over time, often naturally come to appreciate each other greatly. The word love is sometimes not too strong.

Likewise, those we happen to be involved with in the life of our local church, week by week, month by month, year by year, become comfortably familiar. Scripture is filled with the vocabulary of "brothers" and "family" in a spiritual sense. (Additionally, churches reinforce the home-based responsibility of biological or adopted children to obey and honor their parents; parents gain assistance in rearing their children in the nurture of the Lord.) It's inevitable that we will develop affection, quite naturally, with some in our church. They often have their quirks, but eventually we find that we enjoy or appreciate them. I've seen it in a Sunday school class of adults whose core group had met weekly for more than twenty years. I've seen it in choir members who faithfully practiced (yes, even with that soprano who couldn't keep the melody straight). Those who love with affection need agapē because jealousy can wreck it. Siblings can fight and start hating. In the crucible of the local congregation, the adage "love covers a multitude of sins" is proven true (1 Pet 4:8; see Prov 10:12).

Eros. By eros is meant being in love. This is not the same as making love or having sex. Like animals, we humans are capable of joining our bodies with another without anything like the state of being in love. Indeed, in contemporary, over-sexualized Western culture, we have too often supposed that sexual attraction is the same as eros. Plenty of people are filled with sexual desire; they demand the right to casual sex. True eros focuses on the single person one is in love with. Eros is preoccupied with the loved one. Like Jacob who served Laban for seven years to marry Rachel, nothing else mattered. The time "seemed like only a few days to him because of his love for her" (Gen 29:18). Eros wants to "know" the loved one backwards and forwards. Not by accident does the Hebrew of the Old Testament use the verb know (yada) for sexual intimacy, as early as Genesis 4:1.

There is no necessary interplay between being in love, making love, and marriage. For most of human history (and in many cultures even today), marriages were arranged by parents, then came sex, and then eros developed. This was no doubt the case when Paul exhorted Christian husbands to love their wives, that is, to stay in love with them (because sexual desire can fade). The biblical teaching on the permanence of marriage as a life-long covenant makes sense only if eros is interwoven with agapē—sacrificial, self-giving love for a lifetime.

Conversely, some couples have fallen deeply in love, but rightly they never marry or make love. For example, one may already be married, and so the couple sacrifices their being in love for the sake of obeying God. Or one may have a divine call to remain single. A local congregation is part of God's provision for how individual disciples navigate being in love. If we fall in love with someone who might be a suitable marriage partner, fellow church members are an important resource to help us evaluate whether Christian marriage is right. Further, the congregation ought to encourage married members to keep on being in love. Churches are surely right to insist on counseling assistance to the married who say they are no longer in love. That's why eros must stay intertwined with agapē.

Friendship. In the sense used here, "friends" have intentionally chosen each other. Unlike affection and eros (which are universal), friendship isn't essential for a successful life. Typically, such friendship begins because two persons discover a shared interest and they want to spend time together based on that common interest. This may take the form of sportsmanship (fly fishing or duck hunting) or a hobby (knitting or building model trains) or any number of things. Friends of this sort typically withdraw from the larger group. They may become an informal club. They love to hang out and talk shop. What has already been said about accountability partners can be included here. So can the section above about Barnabas, Silas, and Timothy relationships. Certainly, such friendships can play an important role in our journey toward godliness.

Friendships between two or three Christian women may be "secular," for example, if it is based on enjoyment of French cooking. Christian men may have rewarding friendship based on rebuilding classic cars. But there are also friendships based on something sacred. Think of Ruth and Naomi; David and Jonathan; or Peter, James, and John. When we choose a friend and develop that relationship, something spiritual can happen. But great care must be taken to intertwine friendship love, a natural, with agapē. We dare not run the risk of becoming arrogant or exclusivist in our friends. Others can easily get hurt and misunderstand us. We don't want secondary issues to rupture friendships. What we do want is to experience the reality of Proverbs 17:17: "A friend loves at all times, and a brother is born for a difficult time."

Reflective Questions

- How important has fellowship or community with others been in your spiritual journey?
- Have you ever sought out individuals in your church to connect with? Why or why not?
- How should local churches strengthen natural friendships, marriages, and parenting?

MISSION IN COMMUNITY (SUPPER WITH THE SON)

Christ invites us to feast with him by joining with others on the mission he has entrusted to his people. We "sup with the Son" by carrying out the great commission: to bear witness to him in the power of the Spirit and to make disciples from all the nations (Matt 28:19–20; Acts 1:8).

Each local congregation is responsible to determine how it will fulfill this commission. Local churches are often assisted in this task by affiliated agencies. Congregations within a denominational structure will support various mission agencies that the denomination considers part of its calling. This may take the form of financial support for evangelistic endeavors, nationally or internationally. Or it may take the form of sending out some of its own members in special projects, such as planting a new congregation or short-term evangelistic opportunities either locally or far away.

The Mission of Witness

As he was about to ascend to the Father, Jesus commissioned the apostles, once they were empowered by the Spirit, to be his witnesses "in Jerusalem, in all Judea and Samaria, and to the end of the earth" (Acts 1:8). Although in the original setting our Lord was speaking quite literally—and Acts is the historical record of how the first Christians carried out this commission—his words have been widely understood as a paradigm for each local congregation. Every congregation is responsible for bearing witness to Christ in ever-expanding circles: locally, regionally, and globally.

"In Jerusalem." For a few years the first followers of Jesus happily concentrated their witness in their home city. This was obviously the right thing to do. Their proclamation of Jesus as Lord and Savior came about in a variety of ways. First, their leaders publicly proclaimed Christ. Peter's sermon on Pentecost is a well-known example (Acts 2). Second, Christ's ministry of caring for those with grave needs was extended. Healing miracles occurred (Acts 3); believers sold their capital assets to serve the poor (Acts 4). Third, they gladly endured opposition for the sake of Christ (Acts 5). Fourth, these followers of Jesus demonstrated new attitudes and practices about embracing and serving those different from the majority (Acts 6).

Our Jerusalem. The message of the good news has not changed. The importance of gospel proclamation leading to gospel invitation has not changed.

People have not changed, but culture has changed. Communication has changed. How do we as a local church carry out our responsibility to witness to Christ?

- **Our leaders proclaim Christ publicly.** This is done in a variety of ways. Sunday services for the worship of God should regularly include gospel proclamation and invitation. Individuals should, at least from time to time, be given an opportunity to respond to gospel witness. Some congregations schedule special evangelistic meetings, perhaps in an alternate location. It's also important for leaders of a church to provide every-member evangelism equipping. Peter the apostle wrote that believers are to be "ready at any time to give a defense to anyone who asks you for a reason for the hope that is in you" (1 Pet 3:15). Many outstanding resources, such as Evangelism Explosion, are available to teach members ways to witness for Christ effectively.
- **We care for those with grave needs.** Miraculous healings may not often be part of a church's witness, but we still care for the sick and the needy among us. Historically, Christians were the ones who organized to build hospitals. While single congregations can't fund an entire hospi-

tal, several congregations together can bear witness to Christ through health care. Of course, there are always opportunities at the local church level to serve those who are sick and in need of support.

- **We endure opposition for the sake of Christ.** Around AD 200 the Christian theologian Tertullian wrote, "The blood of the martyrs is the seed of the church." He meant that when persecution rises and Christians remain steadfast, many onlookers will admire and turn to follow Christ. While this maxim is not always true—Christianity has been blotted out in some places—it is encouraging. The risen Christ promised, "Be faithful to the point of death, and I will give you the crown of life" (Rev 2:10).
- **We demonstrate new attitudes and practices of inclusion.** The first congregation in Jerusalem figured out how to include needy widows from different cultures in its ministry (Acts 6). Later, the apostles figured out how to be multicultural, welcoming first Samaritans and then Gentiles into full fellowship. (Acts 15 describes the council of apostles and elders at which this was officially embraced.) Paul longed for believers in Galatia to embrace in practice what was theoretically true, that in Christ racial distinctions, gender distinctions,

and socioeconomic differences should be entirely secondary in the life of a congregation (Gal. 3:28).

"In Judea and Samaria." The first Christians left their city only when they were forced out by persecution (Acts 8). Yet they finally proclaimed Christ throughout the region of which Jerusalem was a part. From the viewpoint of the Roman government, "Judea and Samaria" was one administrative district; from a cultural perspective, however, the two were ethnically diverse. Jews and Samaritans distrusted each other (John 4:9). About the same time the early church was forced out of Jerusalem, an Ethiopian official heard and received the good news. While the record is brief (Acts 8), it is proof that Jesus's first followers took seriously his command to witness regionally.

Our Judea and Samaria. Local churches are responsible to think and act regionally in evangelistic emphasis. For example, in the early centuries churches in a single geographical region combined forces to comprise a diocese under the administrative leadership of a bishop. Among other responsibilities, bishops assisted local congregations in carrying out their responsibility to witness for Christ throughout the entire region (see Acts 19:10 for an example from Paul's ministry). Other models have also been developed throughout the centuries for regional witness and service. Some churches work in voluntary associations to carry out the work of evangelism and ministry. Other congregations partner with parachurch organizations that target evangelistic efforts to specific groups. Examples include campus ministries designed to reach high school or college students, or prison ministries that proclaim the good news to those incarcerated (Luke 4:18).

Again, it is the responsibility of each local congregation to think, plan, and pray about how to be involved in reaching its "Judea-and-Samaria." We do not have the freedom to ignore this part of Jesus's commission.

"To the end of the earth." In response to the prompting of the Spirit, the church in Antioch commissioned the first "international missionaries," Paul and Barnabas (Acts 13:2–4). The rest of the Acts describes how this mission proceeded, concluding with Paul's arrival in Rome, the imperial capital. Churches had been planted in multiple provinces; Jesus's letters to the seven churches in the province of Asia show the state of these congregations about the end of the first century (Rev 2–3). Christian history is largely the account of how congregations continued to spread until the church became the global presence that it is today.

Our end of the earth. No local congregation can go it alone in the challenge of global witness. There are many ways it can seek to fulfill Christ's command.

- **Partner with mission-sending agencies.** Many parachurch institutions and denominational boards exist for global evangelization. Local churches, whether denominational or not, now have plenty of opportunities to partner with specialized agencies. Some agencies target specific parts of the world. (China and Africa were favorite focal regions in previous centuries.) Other agencies focus on a particular kind of evangelistic witness, for example, Bible translation for language groups that do not yet have Scripture available.

- **Provide opportunities for members to be sent internationally.** Clearly the Lord is still in the business of calling and sending disciples out from their churches, just as Paul and Barnabas were sent by the Antioch church. This may take the form of teaching people about God's call, providing opportunities—including financial support—for members to be sent as career missionaries, or providing occasions for teams from a local church to be sent for short-term evangelism or ministry. Jesus himself made a connection between fulfilling this aspect of global witness and his return: "This good news of the kingdom will be proclaimed in all the world as a testimony to all nations, and then the end will come" (Matt 24:14).

The Mission of Making Disciples

Making converts is only part of the great-commission responsibility Jesus gave his people. The second part of the commission is to make disciples, that is, learners or followers of Jesus (Matt 28:19-20). Individuals may certainly engage in one-on-one discipleship, as the previous chapter on companionship in community makes clear. Yet local churches make disciples most readily. In the Lord's understanding, discipleship focused on "baptizing them . . . [and] teaching them to observe everything I have commanded."

The verb translated "make disciples" (Greek, manthanō) and the noun "disciple" (Greek, mathētēs) both carry the essential idea of learner or follower. Not only do we endeavor to take the gospel to persons so that they will repent and believe, we want them to become fully devoted followers of Jesus. In a sense, that's what this book is about: the process by which converts become mature, godly followers of Jesus.

The first generation of Christians made disciples in churches in two primary ways. First, spiritual leaders taught the people the Word of God. "They devoted themselves to the apostles' teaching" (Acts 2:42); "I did not avoid declaring to you the whole plan of God" (Acts 20:22). Second, leaders wrote letters of instruction and encouragement. Of Paul's thirteen letters, nine were written to local congregations (all except the letters to Titus, Timothy, and Philemon). The rest of the Epistles were likewise sent to churches (except for 2 John and 3 John).

This shows that the primary responsibility for making disciples lies with local churches. The pattern for such discipleship is found in Paul's challenge to Timothy: "What you have heard from me in the presence of many witnesses, commit to faithful men who will be able to teach others also" (2 Tim 2:2).

Discipleship within a local church. Local churches fulfill their responsibility to make disciples of their own people in many ways.

- **The teaching ministry of "the pulpit."** One hallmark is the faithful teaching of God's Word, an emphasis recovered in the Reformation of the sixteenth century. We have already seen (in the chapter on spiritual gifts) that the Spirit's gift of teaching has been given to some individuals for the benefit of the entire church. The line between "teaching" and "preaching" in Sunday worship is sometimes blurry. For present purposes, it's enough to recognize that when the Word is proclaimed faithfully, Sunday after Sunday, those who listen and apply that Word will grow as disciples.
- **Christian education venues.** A variety of approaches come to mind. Sunday school has been a primary opportunity for teaching children and youth because many affordable published curriculums are available for appropriate developmen-

tal stages. For adults, sometimes teaching the Bible on Sundays has been organized by age group (young adults, senior adults, etc.). For these, discussion and application of Scripture can be tailored to the life stage of those involved. In other churches, age-group organization is avoided. More recently, many churches are set up so that community groups are the primary vehicle for discipleship. For both these and adult Sunday school, sometimes printed studies have been used as a guideline for teaching, and sometimes each group has crafted its own approach under the supervision of the church's spiritual leaders.

- **Special discipleship intensives.** Many churches plan and carry out special times of teaching biblical truth. Sometimes these are targeted toward a specific age group, for example "biblical principles for raising godly children." Sometimes they are topical, such as "learning biblical principles for finances and stewardship." Sometimes they are appropriate for the entire congregation, for instance, "a weekend study of Genesis."

Discipleship beyond a local church. Local churches may band together, in denominational structures and otherwise, to help fulfill their responsibility to make disciples in other ways. A few important examples may be noted.

- **Private Christian schools.** Many churches, both in past ages and more recently, have felt obligated to provide education alternatives beyond what public education provides. Sometimes the motive has been the perceived poor quality of public schools; often the motive has been to provide education more consistent with biblical values, for example, emphasizing humans as created by and responsible to the Creator rather than as products of evolution that did not involve God in any way. It is a matter of some irony that the first compulsory public schools in North America were based on the "Old Deluder Satan Act" of 1647, in the Massachusetts Bay Colony, so that children could be taught to read the Bible and thus defeat Satan, the old deluder.
- **Private Christian colleges and universities.** The earliest universities in Europe developed from cathedral schools or monastic schools. The oldest universities (such as the Universities of Paris and Oxford) prepared men for the clergy and other professions. The earliest American universities, Harvard and Yale, were established for the same reason. Christian

denominations have often funded colleges for young adults from their own denominational heritage. Although such schools might not formally call themselves disciple-making schools, that is what many of them are. Additionally, through the Bible-college movement in the United States, many future pastors and missionaries have been equipped.

- **Seminaries for clergy.** Theological seminaries are professional schools that equipped persons for Christian ministry, just as law schools and medical schools offer professional preparation. However, in addition to providing biblical and theological knowledge and ministry skills, seminaries also give attention to discipleship. It's increasingly acknowledged that spiritual formation—discipleship, maturing in godliness—is as important, if not more important, than professional knowledge. So critical has the role of seminaries been that many mission agencies have built campuses (and equipped faculty members) around the world so that indigenous pastors will be able to lead their congregations as fully committed followers of Christ.

Reflective Questions

- How have you fulfilled the commission to be a witness for Christ? Has your church helped?
- In what ways does your church do the work of making disciples for Christ?
- Does "Jerusalem, Judea and Samaria, and the end of the earth" play a role in your church?

SERVICE IN COMMUNITY (SUPPER WITH THE SON)

Christ invites us to feast with him by joining with others in loving our neighbors as ourselves by serving them. We "sup with the Son" by carrying out the great commandments: to love God wholly and to love neighbors well (Mark 12:28-31, citing Deut 6:4–5 and Lev 19:18).

The previous chapter drew attention to the great commission that Jesus gave us: to bear witness and to make disciples. Now we move to a closely intertwined theme. While individuals can and do love others through serving them, that service will be multiplied as we work alongside others in our congregation.

This chapter thus serves as a fitting capstone for the overall focus of this book about growing in godliness, for love lies at the heart of true service. We have seen the centrality of love all along. Without love, we will not succeed in glorifying God as our chief end; love is the greatest of the virtues; it is essential if the relationships we are developing—whether affection, eros, or friendship—are to be enduring. And so it is that love is required if serving one another (and those outside our church community) is to be anything other than a dreadful duty.

Examples in Scripture of Service Motivated by Love

Consider how serving others worked in the Old Testament, in the life of Jesus, and among the first Christians. First, many Old Testament laws were about helping others and being sure they were treated fairly. Thus, Exodus 22:1–4 provides guidelines for protecting against theft; Exodus 23:21–25 offers rules for just treatment of immigrants, widows, orphans, and the poor—categories of vulnerable persons that we readily understand more than three thousand years later. There are narratives that describe how love for neighbor was applied practically, such as Boaz's compassion for Ruth, a poor foreign widow, or Solomon's wise justice concerning competing claims of two prostitutes for a child. The burden of the prophets was often about what we would call social justice. The Lord requires his people "to act justly, to love faithfulness, and to walk humbly with your God" (Mic 6:8).

When Jesus returns to judge the nations, he will evaluate persons on the extent to which they fed the hungry, sheltered the homeless, clothed those without, cared for the sick, and visited prisoners (Matt

25:35–40). Throughout the Gospels, our Lord carried out a ministry not only of proclaiming the good news but also of healing the sick and driving out evil spirits. He commissioned the Twelve to do the same (Matt 10:1, 5–8). They did so, and Acts reports that they kept on serving others as a continuation of Jesus's ministry. Cripples were healed. Poor widows were assisted with food distribution. A large offering was gathered from Gentile churches to help believers suffering in Jerusalem. This emphasis continues throughout the Epistles, and Paul's letter to Philemon is all about just treatment for a runaway slave.

Service as Spiritual Warfare

Jesus's good deeds included defeating evil spirits. He recognized that satanic powers were at work trying to get him to fail. He claimed that his exorcism ministry was evidence of the presence of God's kingdom and that he was disarming the "strong man," the devil (Luke 11:20–22). Acts shows that the apostles continued to defeat evil spirits directly in the name of Jesus. Paul's teaching on spiritual warfare is a sober reminder that all disciples of Jesus struggle against cosmic powers of darkness, spiritual forces of evil (Eph 6:10–17). The epistles regularly remind us of the reality of evil spirits opposing the ways of God.

With a Western, science-driven mindset, we may have difficulty acknowledging the reality of evil forces at work to oppose the gospel and works of loving service. We do so at our own peril. Evil motivated by fallen humans certainly accounts for much evil in the world, but the devil and his demons (yes, we must accept that these are not just metaphors; they are personal evil powers) are at work to keep the darkness in place. That's why churches historically have maintained exorcism as part of their spiritual arsenal. Multitudes of missionaries to developing countries have attested that their encounters with pagan religions—various forms of animism or Hinduism, for example—have demonstrated the vile reality of satanic power. When we do good works of loving service in Jesus's name today, we should not be surprised that we are struggling against more than merely human evil. Entrenched evils—racial discrimination, degradation of women, and the scourge of drug and alcohol addiction, for instance—cannot be accounted for as merely human evils. If they were, then education and financial resources would solve these problems. Followers of Jesus are called on to enter such realms of bondage with trembling awareness that Satan opposes the light and that Jesus, the light of the world, must demonstrate—through his people—that his kingdom is coming. As we engage in loving service, we continue to pray, "Your kingdom come, your will be done on earth as it is in heaven" (Matt 6:10–11).

Examples of Service Motivated by Love in Christian History

Christians have always recognized that our Lord expects us to meet grave human needs, not only within our congregations but outside as well. The emphasis has typically been on serving the poor and the powerless. In medieval Europe, hospitals were sustained by the tireless energies of monks and nuns. Florence Nightingale, the pioneer of modern nursing, was motivated by a call from God. In more recent times both Protestants and Catholics have sponsored hospitals and nurse training. (In my city, the Methodist and Baptist health care systems are in friendly competition for providing excellent, comprehensive care.)

John Wesley, founder of the Methodist movement, led in prison reform and abolitionist movements in eighteenth-century England. He was a friend of John Newton and William Wilberforce, who helped end the slave trade in Britain. (Tragically, many Christians refused to acknowledge the evils of slavery; the Civil War in America is bitter proof of that. And racism has continued to be a thorny problem, even among believers of good will.) Individual churches and whole denominations have regularly worked together in such good-works endeavors as providing orphanages and opposing alcoholism. The Salvation Army is a stellar example of disciples of Jesus called to serve the marginalized. It's no accident that the leader of the Civil Rights movement in the United States was an ordained Baptist minister with pastoral experience, the Rev. Dr. Martin Luther King Jr.

Examples of Service Motivated by Love Today

How then can we love our neighbors as ourselves? There's no end of opportunity for individuals to do good works. Jesus's parable of the good Samaritan is easy proof. However, following the "Jerusalem, Judea and Samaria, and end of the earth" model developed in the previous chapter, we can consider ways congregations may love our neighbors well.

Service based in the local congregation. It's up to each local congregation to be intentional about expressions of service. First is the importance of teaching and challenging God's people about the relationship between faith and good deeds. Growth in Christlikeness means living out the challenge of James 2:26: "Just as the body without the spirit is dead, so also faith without works is dead."

Second, local churches can commit to serve their own members with ongoing, organized ministries or as new needs arise, just as the church in Jerusalem rose to the challenge of providing food for all its widows, whatever their ethnicity (Acts 6). Many churches deploy teams to provide food to shut-ins or members facing illness, hospitalization, or bereavement. Some churches have built ancillary facilities so that their children and youth (and even adults) can learn cooperation through organized sports. (Often these facilities have become places in which children and youth not connected to the church learn cooperation—and hear the good news of salvation in Christ.) Still another example is a men's organization to meet house-repair needs. It speaks volumes when a roof is replaced or lawns are mowed or plumbing is fixed in the name of Christ.

Third, local churches can consider how to meet needs in their "Jerusalem." Much depends on the economic and cultural setting of the church. Organized ministries, however, are ways to express Christ's love. If immigrant populations live nearby, churches face all sorts of opportunities, including classes that teach English. If there are school children who need help with studies, after-school tutoring is certainly doable. If there are homeless persons in the neighborhood, once-a-week soup kitchens extend the love of Christ; if one church joins with six others in the neighborhood, that covers weekly "daily bread" for those without. Many congregations encourage members to designate part of their giving toward a benevolence fund, which a designated leader or group administers.

Service beyond what local congregations alone can do. Human need, much of it desperate, never disappears. The effects of sin always devastate lives; loving service will always be a part of the calling of churches. Jesus acknowledged this offhandedly: "You always have the poor with you, and you can do what is good for them whenever you want" (Mark 14:7). As with witness, so with service: some needs require cooperation among congregations.

Locally. Many parachurch organizations have come about because Christ's love compelled a visionary founder to act and organize for service. William Booth founded the Salvation Army—now a global entity that is part church and part charitable organization for the poor. (Once I served on the pastoral staff of a church in a city in which most churches of multiple denominations supported the Salvation Army to coordinate ministry to stranded travelers. We were located on a major highway where cross-country travelers sometimes ran out of food and fuel.) Organizations to assist refugees or immigrant populations can be served by local churches. In many cities, rescue missions meet the needs of the homeless, often addicts and those with mental disease. They always need the financial and hands-on help from churches in their cities. Similarly, other ministries have focused on helping battered women or those enslaved by sex trafficking. Such organizations always welcome input from individuals and congregations.

Regionally. Sometimes serious needs arise because of natural disasters, such as tornadoes, earthquakes, and hurricanes. While government agencies address such crises, many churches have organized to provide on-the-ground disaster relief. Denominations have arranged training, trailers, and provisions. People resources and life-sustaining services can move quickly to those deeply affected. Local churches are called on to be intentional about how they can become part of such efforts.

The growth of the social work movement—now professionalized, as with nursing—has brought about another dimension in which local churches offer support beyond their own boundaries. Jane Addams, the mother of social work, was an American Christian whose tireless work was motivated by the gospel. (She won the Nobel Peace Prize in 1931.) Social-work education is necessary today to gain licensure (just as in the case of nursing), but Christian-based social-work programs are thriving. One of the commonly used foundational expressions is that "Jesus was the first social worker." Some churches have employed licensed social workers as part of their ministry staff.

In the 1960s many churches rightly embraced the Civil Rights movement in the name of justice for Christ's sake. Part of the church's witness to the good news of Christ is responding well to injustice. The specific issues put forth in the name of social justice change from time to time. Environmental concerns, the death penalty, racism and discrimination, access to health care and education, concerns for the elderly, and labor conditions are prominent today. Not every church can address each of these matters; they must choose where they can best show the love of Christ.

One matter worth mentioned is the challenge of defining what constitutes a biblically warranted issue of social justice. Two noteworthy examples today are abortion rights and same-sex marriage rights, in which the cultural consensus about what is just is opposed to the historic understanding of Scripture and to the ways Christians have traditionally understood these issues. Thus, for example, the universal consensus of all cultures until the end of the twentieth century was that marriage is assumed to be heterosexual. In the twenty-first century, championing same-sex marriage has become all about social justice for many.

Globally. It can be difficult for individual believers and for individual congregations to know how to express the love of Christ by meeting needs halfway across the globe. Yet there are ways to get involved. The easiest way is through financial sacrifice. It's easy these days to find faith-based organizations who have targeted chronic needs and to support them generously. Many developing nations are in desperate need of ways to house and educate orphans, especially in regions torn by long-term war.

Some organizations have gone into regions with well-thought-out agricultural programs that enable rural people, often isolated, to learn farming techniques that can make a significant difference in providing sustainable food. (I once observed a model farm operation in a tropical Asian country in which farmers were taught how to dig fish tanks, line them, stock them, and then market the fish at a profit.) There are also plenty of opportunities for short-term medical trips to chronically underserved areas. (Some missionary agencies have incorporated clinics into their ministries.)

As another example, Christians with success in business and finance have observed the success of microloans and targeted developing-world opportunities to help people rise out of poverty. Microloans are small, short-term loans with little or no interest to poor, self-employed individuals so that they can go into business—or expand a business—and support themselves and others. Women, for example, might buy a sewing machine so that they can make and sell garments; men might buy equipment so that they can make bricks from local clay.

The possibilities are endless. There is no shortage of ways to express Christ's love though service. Again, we must take care that we heed the ancient words of James: "If a brother or sister is without clothes and lacks daily food, and one of you says to them, 'Go in peace, stay warm and be well fed,' but you don't give them what the body needs, what good is it?" (Jas 2:15–16).

Only in relationship with other Christians will we truly fulfill the great commandments: love God and love our neighbors. Jesus provided the example of loving service to others, and Christians have historically been involved in loving service to society at large (such as hospitals and orphanages). The specific issues that we focus on in the twenty-first century are changing from earlier days. Together, congregations decide on matters of ministry and social justice. Our calling to journey toward Christlike maturity cannot be separated from our calling as participants in a specific Christian community that serves as Christ himself served.

Reflective Questions

- To what extent should a local church meet the needs of its own people ahead others?
- In what ways does your church serve the needs of outsiders in your city or community?
- Is there a new area of loving service that you would like to engage? How will you proceed?

Milton Keynes UK
Ingram Content Group UK Ltd.
UKHW020038191023
430900UK00018B/1392